101 Essential
Word for Windows
Tips

Herbert L. Tyson

 Books

Greensboro, North Carolina

Editor: Tony Roberts
Interior Design: The Roberts Group

Printed in the United States of America.

10 9 8 7 6 5 4 3 2 1

Library of Congress Cataloging-in-Publication Data
Tyson, Herbert L.
    101 essential Word for Windows tips / Herbert L. Tyson
       p. cm.
    Includes Index
    ISBN 0-87455-266-4
    1. Microsoft Word for Windows (Computer program) 2. Word processing--Computer programs. 3. Desktop publishing--computer programs.   I. Title.
Z52.5.M523T95   1992
652.5'536—dc20   92-13892
                                            CIP

COMPUTE Books, 324 West Wendover Avenue, Suite 200, Greensboro, North Carolina 27408, is a General Media International Company and is not associated with any manufacturer of personal computers.

Word for Windows is a registered trademark of Microsoft Corp.

Contents

Formatting Tips

Display Tips

Printing and Graphics Tips

Help Tips

Customization Tips

Introduction

What exactly is a tip? I'm not entirely certain. Some concepts that I originally thought were tips turned out to be exercises in obscure trivia (they're not in this book). Other procedures that I thought were intuitive and obvious turned out to be hot tips. The value of a tip, like beauty, is in the eye of the beholder.

Over the past several months, I've made it my business to *notice* how I and others work with *Word for Windows*. I've tried to be aware of what I do and how I do it. I've also listened carefully to others to discover what they find useful in their day-to-day work. Through all of this, I hope I've managed to compile a list of tips that can help *Word for Windows* users of all levels.

Why a tip book? Well, it's a matter of time. Few people have time to read the *Word for Windows* manual cover to cover. Most people are too busy to scroll through every nook and cranny of the help system looking for unnoticed nuggets. But I *made* the time to study the documentation, and I logged hours working with every *Word for Windows* feature to learn the best approaches for a variety of tasks. Now that I've completed the legwork, you can share my discoveries as you need them, simply by flipping through this book.

I've tried to impose some organization on this information, but because there's no shortage of overlap among *WinWord* concepts, it was difficult to pigeonhole every tip into one of six categories. But, this book is short, sweet, and filled with pictures, so it won't be *that* difficult to thumb through.

I've classified the tips into the following rough categories:

Editing—Tips 1–30, on navigating through the program and on selecting, copying, deleting, and moving text

Formatting—Tips 31–60, on changing the appearance of text

Display—Tips 61–69, on setting up the screen and document windows

Printing and graphics—Tips 70–76, on printing and manipulating pictures

Help—Tips 77–84, on using the *WinWord* interface and help system

Customizing—Tips 85–101, on changing the *WinWord* interface and how it works

Conventions and Definitions

In working with *WinWord*, you'll find that many operations are akin to a dialog. You ask *WinWord* to do something, and it responds. Sometimes it requests additional information. In presenting this conversation on paper, I want to make clear who says what.

Messages and prompts from *Word for Windows*

When *Word for Windows* sends you a message or prompts you for further action, This book will resent those message and prompts by showing you the dialog box or displaying the message in *italic*. For, example, *Do you want to save the global glossary and command changes?* is a frequent message from *WinWord*.

Text typed by you

When the dialog calls for you to type something, this book will show that in **bold**. You might be instructed to type the name of a style such as **heading 4**.

Keys and key combinations

When mentioning keys, this book uses the names as they appear on the keyboard: Enter, Shift, Ctrl, Alt, Esc (or Escape), Caps Lock. Key combinations are shown by connecting all components of the combination with hyphens: Ctrl-S, Ctrl-Shift-G, Ctrl-Alt-Shift-Enter, and so on. Key combinations are entered by holding down all of the indicated *shift* state keys (Alt, Ctrl, and Shift), and then pressing the main key part of the assignment. For example, to press Ctrl-Shift-F9 (Unlink Field), press and hold the Ctrl and Shift keys with one hand, and tap the F9 key with the other hand. Don't try to press all three elements of the combination at the same instant. It's almost impossible to do, and it isn't what the computer wants anyway.

Key sequences

Sometimes, *WinWord* needs a sequence of keys rather than a key combination. Key sequences are indicated like this: Alt-O O V (Tools Options View). Here, Alt-O O V means for you to press Alt-O, followed by O, and then followed by V. Release the Alt key after pressing the first O.

Mouse operations

The mouse is responsible for several comparatively new terms. When you are instructed to **move** the mouse, it means just that. Don't press any buttons—just move the mouse. The term **click** means a single quick press and release of the mouse button (usually the left button).

Double-click means to press and release the mouse button (usually the left button) twice in rapid succession. You can adjust the double-click speed using the Mouse option from the Windows Control Panel. This setting determines how quickly you must double-click so Windows recognizes your action as a double-click rather than as two separate single clicks.

The term **drag** means that you **move** the mouse while holding a button down. The effect of dragging varies by operation. Dragging can expand a selection, cause something to move on screen, or cause an object to change shape.

In some instances, an operation requires both mouse and keyboard actions, for example **Ctrl-Click**. When you see Ctrl-Click, you press a Ctrl key on the keyboard and then Click the mouse's left button. As a concept, Ctrl-Click is ergonomically impoverished. The mouse is supposed to be an intuitive *alternative* to the keyboard, not a linked appendage. But that problem is beyond the scope of this book and might better be addressed by letters to a company at One Microsoft Way.

Menu selections

In many of these tips you will see an instruction like "Select Format Paragraph" or its equivalent key sequence (*Alt-T P*). You can use the mouse or any other shortcut you may have developed to advance to that point, because *how* you invoke the Format Paragraph dialog box isn't as important as what you do once you get there. So, when you see "Select Format Paragraph," feel free to press Alt-T P, or click on the word Format and click again on the word Paragraph, or double-click the upper half of the ruler, or press a Format Paragraph shortcut key, if you've assigned one.

Shortcut for Edit GoTo

■ Selecting Edit GoTo from the keyboard is a difficult task.

Use the status bar.

❶ Position the cursor where you want to start your go-to.

❷ Double-Click anyplace on the status bar.

❸ Type a destination: a bookmark (user-defined or built-in; \page); p1s2, for page 1, section 2; or p4l6 for page 4, line 6.

❹ Press Enter.

At the *Go To:* prompt, you can press F1 for additional valid destinations.

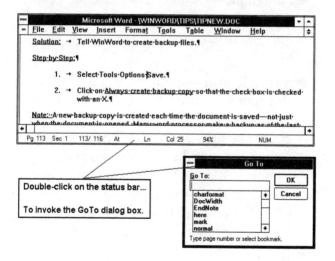

Double-click on the status bar...

To invoke the GoTo dialog box.

Make quick selections with the mouse

■ Touch-up formatting using the keyboard can be tedious.

Use mouse shortcuts to make selections.

Mouse selection shortcuts:

- Word—Double-Click anywhere on the word.
- Line—Click the selection bar (shown in figure).
- Sentence—Ctrl-Click anywhere in the sentence.
- Paragraph—Double-Click the selection bar.
- Document—Ctrl-Click the selection bar.
- Multiple units—perform the indicated shortcut for a unit, but keep the mouse button depressed. Drag the selection to cover the area you want. The selected area will expand unit-by-unit. For example, if you Double-Click on a word, and keep the button pressed after the second click, the selection is expanded word-by-word as you drag the mouse.
- Block—Using the current cursor location as the beginning, move the mouse pointer to where you want the selection to end. Then Shift-Click.

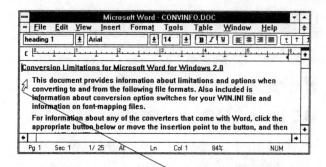

The "selection bar" is the white area to the left of the document in the WinWord text window. When the mouse pointer enters the selection bar, it takes the shape of an arrow (↗). When the mouse pointer is in the text area itself, it takes the I shape.

Select the entire document or pane using the number pad

■ The intuitive way to select the whole document or pane is to press Ctrl-Home (top of document), F8 (extend selection), and Ctrl-End (end of document). While it works, this is the long way around.

Press Ctrl-5 on the number pad.

❶ Position the cursor anywhere in the text area.

❷ Press Ctrl-5 on the number pad.

The Num Lock toggle does not have to be turned on for this to work. This shortcut works only with 5 on the number pad.

Shortcut for selecting text

■ Selecting text can be tiresome—shortcuts are welcome.

Use ExtendSelection.

❶ Position the cursor where you want to start selecting text.

❷ Press F8 (ExtendSelection).

❸ Press the letter or character at the end of the text you want to select. For example, if you want to select up to the end of the sentence, press the period key. If you want to select up to the end of the next paragraph, press Enter. If you want to select up to the next "e," then tap the "E" key. Pressing the space bar extends the selection word-by-word. Pressing the comma key extends the selection up to the next comma, and so on.

If you need to, you can freeze the selection (turn off ExtendSelection) by pressing the Esc key.

More selection shortcuts

■ Moving from keyboard to mouse and back is time-consuming and unproductive.

Use the CUA (Common User Access) selection techniques

Common User Access techniques are common across all Windows and OS/2 Presentation Manager applications.

- Select Character—Shift-Left and Shift-Right.
- Select Word—Ctrl-Shift-Left and Ctrl-Shift-Right.
- Select Line—Shift-Down and Shift-Up.
- Select Paragraph—Ctrl-Shift-Down and Ctrl-Shift-Up.
- Select to end of current line—Shift-End.
- Select to start of current line—Shift-Home.
- Select to end of document—Ctrl-Shift-End.
- Select to start of document—Ctrl-Shift-Home.

When you press the indicated key combinations, *WinWord* selects up to the next boundary of the type indicated. The selection starts at the insertion point. If the insertion point is in the middle of a word, line, or paragraph, then a partial word, line, or paragraph is selected. Thereafter, whole units are selected. Try using one of these techniques in combination with *typing replaces selection* (selected via the Tools Options General menu—see Tip #28). If you want to replace the rest of the current word, for example, press Ctrl-Shift-Right, and start typing the replacement text.

Select an entire table without using the Table menu

■ The Table menu indicates that Alt-5 on the number pad is a shortcut for selecting a table, but sometimes it doesn't work.

The Alt-5 shortcut works only if Num Lock is turned off.

This differs from the shortcut for selecting the whole document, which works regardless of the state of Num Lock.

❶ Position the cursor anyplace in the table.

❷ Make certain that Num Lock is turned off.

❸ Press Alt-5 on the number pad.

Alt-5 with Num Lock turned on is reserved for direct entry of characters by typing Alt plus their ANSI or ASCII codes. This shortcut works only with 5 on the number pad.

Replace the rest of a paragraph without losing formatting

■ When you delete the last part of the current paragraph, it often loses its formatting.

A paragraph's formatting is contained in the paragraph marker. Don't include the paragraph marker in the selection you delete.

❶ Put the cursor where you want to begin the selection.

❷ Press Ctrl-Shift-Down.

❸ Press Shift-Left. This is vital. It deselects the paragraph marker.

❹ Type the replacement text.

Paragraph formatting resides in the paragraph marker. When you delete the paragraph marker between two paragraphs, the two paragraphs are merged. The resulting paragraph keeps the formatting of the second paragraph.

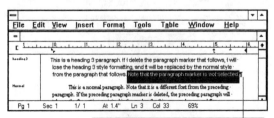

When deleting to the end of a paragraph, be careful not to delete its paragraph marker. Doing so causes the two paragraphs to merge, using the formatting of the latter paragraph.

Move paragraphs using the keyboard

■ Moving a paragraph ordinarily requires four or more steps, depending on how you do it.

Use the Move Paragraph keys.

❶ Put the cursor in the paragraph you want to move.

❷ Press Alt-Shift-Up to swap the current paragraph with the preceding one or Alt-Shift-Down to swap the current paragraph with the paragraph that follows.

❸ Continue to press Alt-Shift-Up or Alt-Shift-Down, to push the selected paragraph along.

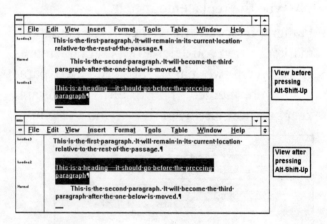

Move paragraphs using the mouse

■ The intuitive method, selecting the paragraph, cutting it to the clipboard, and then pasting it to the new location, requires too many steps.

Use Drop and Drag.

❶ Double-Click the mouse in the selection bar for the paragraph you want to move.

❷ Position the mouse on the selected paragraph, then press and hold the left button.

❸ While holding the left button, drag the selection icon to a new location.

❹ Release the left button to complete the move or drop.

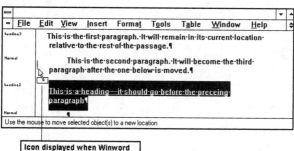

Icon displayed when Winword is using "drag and drop" to move text.

Insert an em dash or other special characters

■ It's neither easy nor intuitive to remember that Alt-0151 (with Num Lock on) is an em dash. It's the same problem with other special characters.

Use the glossary and F3.

❶ Toggle Num Lock On.

❷ Hold down the Alt key and type 0 1 5 1 on the numeric keypad. This enters the ANSI code for an em dash.

❸ Select the resulting character (press Shift-Left).

❹ Select Edit Glossary from the menu.

❺ Type — (two ordinary dashes, with no space between them, the common substitute for an em dash).

❻ Press Alt-D (for define). If you already have something else assigned to "—," you can either select Yes to redefine, or back up and use something else for an em dash.

❼ That done, now you can use "—" as a shortcut for the em dash. The beauty of using "—" is that you can type what you're used to typing, and then press F3 to convert it into a real em dash.

This technique can be applied to other special characters as well: 0150 is an en dash; 0149 is a bullet; 0147 and 0148 are directional double quotation marks; and 0145 and 0146 are directional single quotation marks. I leave it to you to invent the shortcuts to use. For a more useful implementation of directional quotes, however, see the NEWMACROS.DOC file that comes with *WinWord* 2. An em dash is a dash the width of a capital letter M; an en dash—a narrower dash—is the width of a capital letter N.

Insert accented foreign characters

■ If you rarely use foreign characters, the Insert Symbol dialog box may provide all the utility you need (see Tip #22). If you occasionally need to type whole passages in a foreign language, but lack the facility or motivation to convert to a foreign keyboard, Insert Symbol is a painfully slow route to travel.

Use the glossary, forming 2-character glossary names that comprise the accent and the letter you want to use. For example, .e for é, 'i for ì, and ^u for û.

❶ Toggle Num Lock On.

❷ Hold down the Alt key and type **0 2 3 3** on the numeric keypad. This enters the ANSI code for an é.

❸ Select the resulting character (press Shift-Left).

❹ Select Edit Glossary from the menu.

❺ Type **.e** (period followed by a lower case e).

❻ Press Alt-D (for define).

❼ Now, when you want to type an é, **.e** and press F3. The word **habl.e**, for example, becomes *hablé*.

If you use Insert Symbol to produce your accented characters (instead of Alt-number pad combinations), beware of the Normal Text font. Glossaries take on formatting of the item you select. So, set the character font of your foreign characters to your normal font or you will have to insert them as plain text, which requires using Edit Glossary rather than F3 to expand glossary items.

Size a frame with the mouse

■ Resizing a frame using Format Frame is formidable and unintuitive.

Use the mouse.

❶ If you are not already in Page Layout view, select View Page Layout.

❷ Click the mouse left button outside the framed area.

❸ Click the mouse left button inside the framed area. This will reveal eight sizing handles.

❹ To change height and width at the same time, drag one of the corner handles. To drag a corner, position the mouse so that the mouse pointer shape becomes a diagonal double-arrow, and hold down the left button. Move the mouse in the directions indicated by the mouse pointer until the frame is the size you want.

❺ To change height or width only, drag one of the top, bottom, or side handles. Position the mouse so that the mouse pointer shape is a vertical or horizontal double-arrow. Drag the mouse until the frame is the size you want.

Frames are used for pictures, objects, and text that needs to be manipulated in ways not permitted by ordinary techniques. Once you have framed part of a word document, the framed item can be

moved and resized to create special effects, such as
text wrapping around a graphic or dropped capi-
tals. For additional help with frames, see Tips #43
and #60.

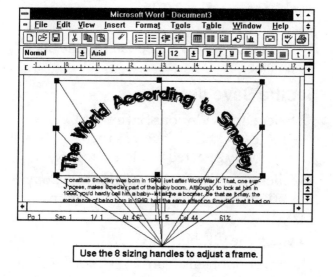

Use the 8 sizing handles to adjust a frame.

Tip #13

Create backup copies of documents with *WinWord*

■ By default, *WinWord* doesn't create backup files.

Set the Save default.

❶ Select Tools Options Save (Alt-O O S; or Alt-O O SS if Save was the previously selected Option category).

❷ Click the **Always Create Backup Copy** option so that the checkbox contains an X.

❸ Click the OK button.

The Save options also can be set from the Save As dialog box. From the Save As dialog box, click on the Options button.

Note also, that a new backup copy is created each time the document is saved—not just when the document is opened. If you revert to a .BAK file during a session in which you've saved many times, the .BAK that exists will only revert you to the file's status just before the most recent File Save.

Once the backup option has been turned on, it remains in effect for this and all future sessions of *WinWord* until you turn it off. See also Tip #87.

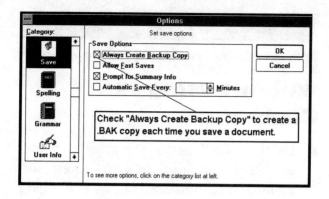

Options

Category:

- Save
- Spelling
- Grammar
- User Info

Set save options

Save Options
- ☒ Always Create Backup Copy
- ☐ Allow Fast Saves
- ☒ Prompt for Summary Info
- ☐ Automatic Save Every: [ ] Minutes

OK
Cancel

Check "Always Create Backup Copy" to create a .BAK copy each time you save a document.

To see more options, click on the category list at left.

Replace selected text without using the Clipboard

■ Using the Clipboard isn't always the quickest way to move or copy text. Moreover, sometimes you already have something in the Clipboard that you don't want to overwrite.

Use the Move or Copy keys.

❶ Select the text you want to move or copy.

❷ Press F2 (the move key) or Shift-F2 (the copy key), depending on whether you want text to remain in its original location.

❸ Select the text you want to replace.

❹ Press Enter.

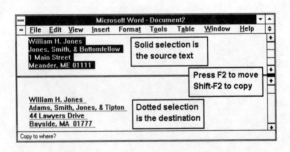

Insert text in front of a table even when a table is at the top of a document

■ If a Word document begins with a table, you cannot insert ordinary text in front of the table. Instead, when you press Ctrl-Home and start typing, text is inserted in the first cell.

Press the column break key.

❶ Press Ctrl-Home to go to the top of the document.

❷ Press Ctrl-Shift-Enter to insert a column break. This forces a carriage return ahead of the table, allowing you to insert text. A single press of Ctrl-Shift-Enter under these circumstances will *not* actually insert a column break—it will insert just a paragraph marker (carriage return). If you press Ctrl-Shift-Enter a second time, however, a column break will be inserted.

Move insertion point to the top of the document (Ctrl-Home). Pressing Enter here just inserts a paragraph marker into the first cell in the table. Pressing Ctrl-Shift-Enter inserts a paragraph marker before the table, allowing you to add text ahead of the table. In this situation, no column break is inserted.

Convert hard carriage returns into word wrapped text

■ Text imported from ASCII files often has hard carriage returns between each line.

Convert hard carriage returns into spaces.

For most ASCII text, this is a three-step process. First, change all double-carriage returns into some unique temporary character. Second, change all remaining carriage returns into spaces. Third, change all of the unique temporary characters into carriage returns.

❶ Select Edit Replace.

❷ In the Find What field, type **^p^p**. Note: you must use a caret followed by a lower case p—an upper case p will not work. The ^p combination is used to search for a carriage return (also called a paragraph marker).

❸ In the Replace With field, type some unique character(s), for example, **&&&**.

❹ Select Replace All.

❺ In the Find What field, delete one of the ^ps.

❻ In the Replace With field, replace &&& with a single space.

❼ Select Replace All.

❽ In the Find What field, replace ^p with **&&&**.

❾ In the Replace With field, replace the space with **^p^p** (or a single **^p** if you prefer only one paragraph marker between paragraphs).

❿ Select Replace All.

Find What:	^p^p		**Find Next**
			Replace
Replace With:	&&&		**Replace All**
			Cancel
☐ Match Whole Word Only	☐ Match Case		

Change paragraphs to a unique string.

Find What:	^p		**Find Next**
			Replace
Replace With:			**Replace All**
			Cancel
☐ Match Whole Word Only	☐ Match Case		

Change line breaks into spaces.

Find What:	&&&		**Find Next**
			Replace
Replace With:	^p^p		**Replace All**
			Cancel
☐ Match Whole Word Only	☐ Match Case		

Change unique strings back into paragraphs. The second paragraph marker is optional.

Make precise selections when recording a macro

■ Selecting precise units while recording a macro is difficult in *WinWord* because the mouse shortcuts are disabled during macro recording.

Use ExtendSelection.

● Press F8 (extend selection) to extend the selection in logically larger units of text. Repeatedly pressing F8 extends the selection as follows:

1 press	Begin selection
2 presses	Word
3 presses	Sentence
4 presses	Paragraph
5 presses	Section (if it's a multi-section document; otherwise, document)
6 presses	Document

Delete a pattern of unknown characters

■ Files imported from other sources, some-times include characters you don't recog-nize. Ordinarily, you'd use Edit Replace to eliminate what you don't want, but not knowing what the characters are, you don't know what to type into the Find What field.

Use the Clipboard.

❶ Select an occurrence of the character(s) you want to eliminate.

❷ Press Shift-Delete to cut the occurrence to the Clipboard.

❸ Select Edit Replace.

❹ In the Find What field, press Shift-Insert to copy the clipboard to the field.

❺ If you want to delete all occurrences, blank the Replace With field; otherwise fill in the replacement text.

❻ Select Replace All.

As used here, the contents of the Clipboard can be pasted into dialog box fill-in areas. You also can copy text from a dialog box fill-in area into the Clipboard. To copy the contents of a text box into the Clipboard, Double-Click the text box of interest to select it, then press Ctrl-Insert, which copies the selected text to the clipboard.

Quickly open the footnote pane for editing in draft view

■ When you want to edit a footnote while in draft view, the tendency is to look in the Edit menu. But, it's not there.

Double-Click on any footnote reference mark.

The long method for editing a footnote is to select View Footnotes and then scroll to the one you want.

● The shortcut method for editing a footnote is to Double-Click on the reference mark of the footnote of interest. If you're in a hurry, you can Double-Click on any footnote reference mark and then scroll to the one you want.

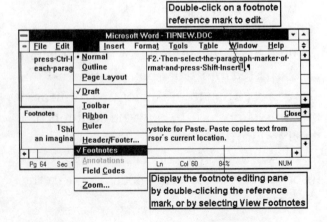

Delete a footnote (or avoid deleting one by accident)

■ When you select View Footnotes and delete the footnote, the reference mark is left behind.

Delete the reference mark.

❶ Position the cursor just ahead of the footnote reference mark in the body of your text.

❷ Press Shift-Right to select the reference mark.

❸ Press the delete key. The reference mark and the footnote are both deleted automatically.

This is as much a precaution as it is a tip. Because deleting the reference mark deletes both mark and footnote, it is easy to delete a footnote by accident.

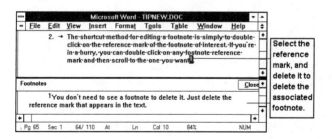

Select the reference mark, and delete it to delete the associated footnote.

Remove hard page breaks from a document

■ Sometimes it's necessary to insert hard page breaks to make a document paginate correctly. But, after revisions, those left-over page breaks are a nuisance. Tools Repaginate Now has no effect on hard page breaks.

Delete them with Edit Replace.

❶ Press Ctrl-Home to go to the top of the document.

❷ Select Edit Replace.

❸ Type ^d or ^12 in the Find What field.

❹ Blank out the Replace With field.

❺ If the document does not contain distinct sections, select Replace All (A). Otherwise, press Enter, and then press R (Replace) for each hard page break you find.

Even though they display differently on the screen, *WinWord* uses the identical ^12 character for section and hard page breaks. In a multi-section document, you must make a decision about each occurrence of a ^12 (form feed character) as to whether it is a page or section break. When the Replace dialog box prompts you for a response, press F (Find Next) to skip section breaks, and press R to make the replacement.

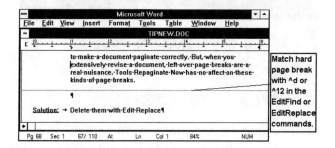

to make a document paginate correctly. But, when you extensively revise a document, left over page breaks are a real nuisance. Tools Repaginate Now has no affect on these kinds of page breaks.

Solution: → Delete them with Edit Replace

Match hard page break with ^d or ^12 in the EditFind or EditReplace commands.

Insert symbols and characters that aren't on the keyboard

■ Looking up symbols in an appendix is a bother. Plus, you don't really see how things are going to look.

Use Insert Symbol.

❶ Put the cursor where you want the symbol to appear.

❷ Select Insert Symbol.

❸ Use the cursor keys (Up, Down, Left, Right) to locate the symbol character you want to use.

❹ If you don't see the symbol or character you want, select Symbols From (Alt-F), and alternately try the MS Line Draw and (Normal Text) fonts.

❺ When the character you want is highlighted, click OK or press Enter. This copies the selected character into your document.

❻ **Caution.** (Normal Text) is not a real font, but is copied as such when you insert a character from that set. If that happens, select the character inserted (Shift-Left) and press Ctrl-Space to restore your normal character formatting.

Even though *WinWord* only displays three fonts by default, you can specify any font in the

Symbol Font text box. Type the name of the font you want, then either click in the symbols area or tab to it. *WinWord* will display the characters associated with the font specified.

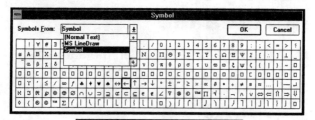

Select the font; then select the character.
Note: Unlike the Character Map, the Insert Symbol utility can insert only one character at a time. To load a number of characters into the clipboard, see the Character Map utility in Windows itself.

Character Map

Return to the last editing spot when you re-edit a file

■ If you repeatedly work on the same file—such as a book or a long report—you usually want to pick up where you left off.

Use GoBack.

❶ Select File Open to open a document.

❷ Press Shift-F5 (Go Back).

Shift-F5 (the Go Back key) toggles among the current cursor location and the last three locations where any editing occurred. The Go Back information is saved each time you close a file. Advanced users can make this procedure automatic by including the GoBack command as part of an AutoOpen macro.

Convert "soft" dates into "hard" dates

■ When you select Insert Date and Time, the resulting date or time is a field code that gets updated each time you print the document. But, a date that changes every time you open a file doesn't help document your work.

Unlink the field.

❶ Put the cursor just ahead of or anywhere on the date field or the date it displays. Field codes can be On or Off—it doesn't matter.

❷ Press Ctrl-Shift-F9.

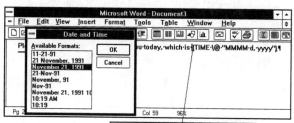

Press Ctrl-Shift-F9 to convert the date field into text. Otherwise, if the field is updated later on, you will be unable to tell what date you were talking about! Note: Insert Time and Date actually inserts a TIME field. But, TIME and DATE are identical in this context.

Undo a typing or formatting mistake

■ Sometimes you delete or reformat text, and you know instantly that you've made an error. Can you reverse your action?

Use Edit Undo.

● *Immediately* after making a mistake, press Alt-Backspace Ctrl-Z. If you wait until you've done something else, Alt-Backspace won't necessarily undo the mistake. For example, if you accidentally assign the wrong style to a section of text, press Alt-Backspace to undo the damage. Alt-Backspace only undoes the last edit performed—it does not maintain an undo stack. Pressing Alt-Backspace a second time just undoes the last undo.

If you have AutoSave turned on (Tools Options Save), and *WinWord* does an automatic save *after* the mistake, but *before* you press Alt-Backspace, Edit Undo is disabled and can't be used to undo the previous edit. So, if you make a mistake, you'd better undo it quickly!

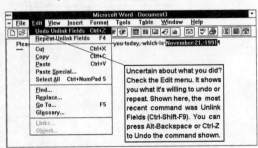

Save a macro without closing it

■ *WinWord* sometimes experiences UAEs (unrecoverable application errors) or GP (general protection) errors. It is especially prone to such problems when you are editing and debugging macros. How can you save your work while editing a macro—without actually closing it?

Use File Save All.

❶ Select File Save All anytime a wave of worry sweeps over you.

❷ Select Yes to the prompt that asks if you want to save changes to the macro.

❸ Select Yes to the prompt that asks if you want to save changes either to global glossary and command changes or to the template that contains the macro.

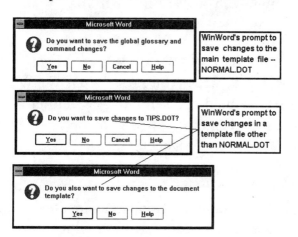

WinWord's prompt to save changes to the main template file -- NORMAL.DOT

WinWord's prompt to save changes in a template file other than NORMAL.DOT

Create automatic numbering systems

■ *WinWord* has several numbering systems, but they either aren't automatic, or you're limited to one system per document.

Use SEQ fields.

❶ Put the cursor where you want a sequence number to appear.

❷ Select Insert Field.

❸ Select Field Code (Alt-C).

❹ Into the Field Code text box, type **seq** *name*, where *name* is a name for the sequence series you want to use. It can be anything meaningful to you such as **seq chart,** or **seq table**.

❺ Press Enter.

❻ Repeat the procedure for each sequence number you want to use in that sequence. If it's something you do frequently, you might consider recording a macro to do it for you.

In Step 5, when you press Enter, *WinWord* inserts a field code that displays either as a number (beginning with 1 the first time you insert a given seq *name*), or as a field code such as {seq list}. Sequence numbers can be modified using switches—that is they can be displayed as numbers, Roman numerals, ordinal numbers, letters, or even restarted at 1 or some other number. While the Insert Field dialog box is displayed, you can press F1 to see these and other options.

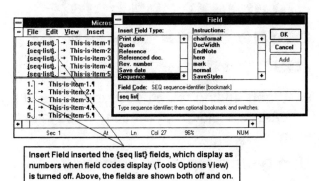

Insert Field inserted the {seq list} fields, which display as numbers when field codes display (Tools Options View) is turned off. Above, the fields are shown both off and on.

Enter text and delete at the same time in Insert mode

■ When adding text in overtype mode, it's easy to accidentally erase text you intend to keep.

Use *typing replaces selection*.

❶ Select Tools Options General.

❷ Turn on Typing Replaces Selection (press Alt-T so that the checkbox is Xed).

❸ With Insert mode on (OVR not visible on the status bar), select the text you want to replace.

❹ Type the replacement text. The first letter you press automatically deletes the selection. Because you're in Insert mode, you won't accidentally overtype any text other than that which you preselected.

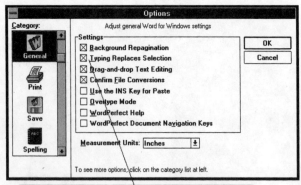

With "Typing Replaces Selection" turned on, selected text is deleted as you begin to type replacement text.

Create a quick place marker

■ Inserting bookmarks is a multi-step process that insists that you name a location. Bookmarks are overkill when all you need is a method to quickly and temporarily mark a spot for return.

Use GoBack.

❶ Put the cursor in the location you want to mark.

❷ Press Backspace once.

❸ Press Alt-Backspace, once. (Steps 2 and 3 create a "false edit." Backspace deletes the preceding character, and Alt-Backspace undoes the delete. The document has not changed, but *WinWord* thinks that it has.)

❹ Shift-F5 (GoBack) can now be used to return the cursor to the false edit location. Shift-F5 toggles the cursor location among the last four locations where editing occurred.

How to insert a tab into a table

■ When you press the Tab key while typing text into a table, *WinWord* skips to the next cell, and does not insert a tab.

Press Ctrl-Tab to insert a tab while in a table.

❶ Put the cursor where you want the tab to appear.

❷ Press Ctrl-Tab.

Shortcut for character formatting

■ When you format a document using a mouse, repeatedly selecting Format Character from the menu becomes tiresome.

Double-Click the blank area on the Ribbon.

❶ Place the cursor where you want to apply character formatting.

❷ Double-Click in the blank area on the Ribbon—any place other than on an icon or list box. The Format Character dialog box will appear.

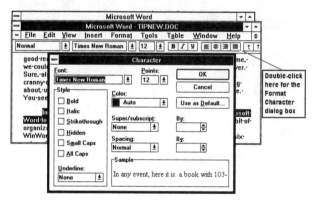

Shortcut for paragraph formatting

■ Selecting Format Paragraph can be mo-
notonous after a while.

**Double-Click the Ruler, anywhere
above the middle line.**

❶ Place the cursor where you want to apply
paragraph formatting.

❷ Double-Click on the Ruler, above the
base line. The Format Paragraph dialog
box will appear.

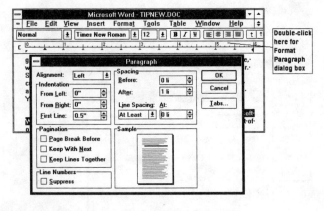

Shortcut for tab formatting

■ Selecting Format Tabs with the keyboard
and then switching to the mouse is inefficient. Even performing the whole operation with a mouse takes more steps than
necessary.

Double-Click on the Ruler, anywhere below the middle line.

❶ Position the cursor where you want to
apply tab formatting.

❷ Double-Click in the lower half of the
Ruler area, on any existing tab or indent
icon. The Format Tab dialog box
appears. You actually can Double-Click
anywhere in the lower half. Confining it
to an existing tab or indent icon,
however, prevents you from accidentally
creating unwanted tab settings.

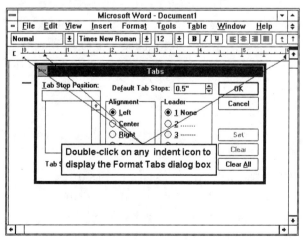

Create superscripts, subscripts, and double underlining without using the menu

■ In *Word for Windows* 1, you could perform speed formatting using the Ribbon. In version 2, some of the commands are gone.

Use alternative shortcuts.

In *Word for Windows* 1, the Ribbon was used for character formatting, and the Ruler was used for paragraph formatting. In version 2, some paragraph-formatting icons and list boxes were moved from the Ruler to the Ribbon to make room for the ToolBar. The Ruler is now just a ruler, containing no icons. To accommodate having moved icons and list boxes from the Ruler onto the Ribbon, Microsoft removed the icons that seemed less useful. Replacement features, along with other keyboard formatting shortcuts, are shown below.

Alternative shortcuts:

- Superscript, use Ctrl-Shift-Equal (on the top row).
- Subscripts, use Ctrl-Equal (same as superscript, but without the shift).
- Double underlining, use Ctrl-D.
- Word-underlining, use Ctrl-W.

- Italic, use Ctrl-I.
- Bold, use Ctrl-B.
- Underlining, use Ctrl-U.
- All capital letters, use Ctrl-A.
- Hidden text, use Ctrl-H.

If you absolutely cannot function without icons for these character-formatting commands, you can modify the ToolBar. The version 1-style icons for underlining variations are contained among the icons, as are the symbols X_2 and X^2 for subscript and superscript, respectively. See Tip #92.

Merge two paragraphs and keep the formatting of the first

■ When you merge two paragraphs by deleting a paragraph marker, the formatting of the second paragraph is applied to the merged result.

Use ResetPara.

❶ If paragraph markers are not visible, press Ctrl-Shift-8 (top row).

❷ Move the cursor to a point just to the left of the paragraph marker in the first paragraph.

❸ Press Ctrl-Shift-Down, twice.

❹ Press Ctrl-Q (this assigns the paragraph formatting in the first paragraph to the entire selection).

❺ Press Ctrl-Shift-Up.

❻ Press the space bar (this replaces the selected paragraph marker with a space, merging the two paragraphs into one).

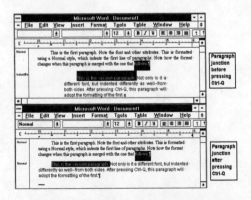

Prevent text from inheriting glossary format

■ When you insert a formatted glossary item, the current text sometimes "inherits" the character *formatting* from the inserted item. For example, make *The New York Times* a glossary entry assigned to nyt. Type **nyt** and press F3, and **nyt** expands into *The New York Times*. But, everything you type after that will be italicized, also.

Trick *WinWord* into memorizing current formatting.

❶ Type the glossary name (the abbreviation).

❷ Press the space bar. The abbreviation and space you type are both formatted using current character attributes and formatting.

❸ Press F3. Despite the space, this will expand the abbreviation.

❹ Press Shift-Right once, and then start typing your new text.

Advanced users can save some work by replacing the built-in ExpandGlossary command with the following macro:

```
Sub MAIN
Insert " "
ExpandGlossary
CharRight 1,1
End Sub
```

Convert footnotes from superscript to numbered list style

■ The default style for footnotes is super-script numbers, and bottom-of-page place-ment. This style is unacceptable for many document types.

Perform global search and replace on the complete footnote set.

❶ When the document is finished, press Ctrl-Home to go to the top of the document, and then select View Footnote (Alt-V F).

❷ Select Edit Replace.

❸ Type ^2 into the *Find What* text box (^2 is the search character for a footnote reference mark).

❹ Type ^m.^t into the *Replace With* text box (^*m* is the replace character for "ditto"; the .^t part adds a period and a tab after each footnote reference number).

❺ Press Alt-H to select character formatting.

❻ Select a Superscript or Subscript value of **None,** and select the same font and point size that's used by the footnote text itself. This forces the search and replace command to change the formatting of the footnote reference mark to match that of the footnote text.

❼ Press Enter.

❽ Press Alt-A (to select Replace All).

❾ If you want hanging indents for your endnotes, press Ctrl-5 (number pad) to select the entire footnote set, and then press Ctrl-T.

❿ To cause your endnotes to print at the end of the document instead of at the bottom of each page, see Tip #38.

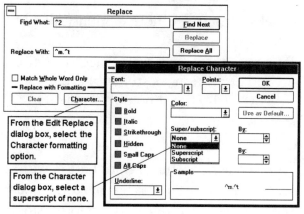

From the Edit Replace dialog box, select the Character formatting option.

From the Character dialog box, select a superscript of none.

Create endnotes instead of footnotes

■ There is no "note type" option in any of the format dialog boxes.

Use the Options button under Insert Footnote.

❶ Select Insert Footnote Options(Alt-I N O)

❷ Choose the appropriate **Place At** option (End of Section, Bottom of Page, Beneath Text, or End of Document).

❸ Press Enter.

❹ Press Esc to avoid inserting a footnote.

The placement of the Options button within the Insert Footnote dialog box makes it appear that you are selecting options for a single footnote. In fact, the **Place At** option affects all footnotes in the document.

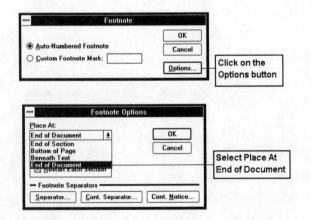

Remove extraneous formatting from a paragraph

■ Formatting in a paragraph can be applied with a style, or can depart from the underlying style in some way. If you try to use Ctrl-S to reformat a paragraph so it conforms strictly to the named style effect, *WinWord* questions your intentions with a barrage of prompts, such as *Do you want to redefine the style based on selection?* or *Replace standard style with selection?*

Use ResetPara (Ctrl-Q).

❶ Put the cursor in the paragraph of interest.

❷ Press Ctrl-Q. This resets all paragraph-level formatting to that of the underlying style. Note, this does not reset character formatting. To reset all variant character formatting, press Ctrl-Space.

A paragraph can be formatted in any of several ways. If you do nothing else to it, a paragraph is formatted according to a style. You can change a paragraph's formatting without giving it a new style name, for example, by changing the line spacing, the indentation, or the tabs. When you do that, you introduce a variant to the assigned style. The ResetPara command removes all paragraph formatting that does not conform to the assigned style.

How to refer to a sequence number

■ To refer to a sequence number (for example, See Tip #40), you have to bookmark it. But, when you refer to the bookmark, the reference itself is treated as a sequence number. It doesn't produce the number to which you refer, and it bumps all subsequent sequence numbers up.

Use a {SEQ sequencename bookmarkname} field.

❶ Select the sequence number to which you want to refer.

❷ Select Insert Bookmark (Alt-I M), and type a name for the bookmark. Choose a name that makes sense in the context. For example, if the item is a regional sales chart, you might name the bookmark **regional**. Also, note the exact name of the sequence being used; for example, {seq chart}.

❸ Position the insertion point where you want the reference to appear, and type something like **See #** to set the reference up.

❹ Select Insert Field (Alt-I D).

❺ Type **ss**. This will select SEQ from the list box of field types.

❻ Press Alt-C to position the cursor in the field text box.

➐ Press Cursor Right once, and type the name of the sequence identifier, **chart**, for example.

➑ Select the appropriate bookmark (**regional**) from the Instructions list box, and press Alt-A to add it to the field text box.

➒ Press Enter or click OK.

Alternatively, press Ctrl-F9 to insert the field characters. Then type **seq treelist elm**, and press F9 to update the field. While this method is fewer steps, many users prefer to use the menu.

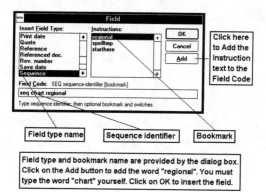

Field type and bookmark name are provided by the dialog box. Click on the Add button to add the word "regional". You must type the word "chart" yourself. Click on OK to insert the field.

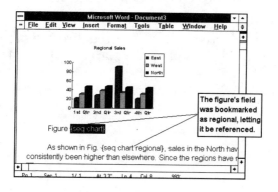

Use the ToolBar Table icon to insert a table

■ When you click on the Table tool icon, a grid appears, but nothing happens.

Expand the grid with the mouse.

❶ Place the cursor where you want the table to appear.

❷ Click on the Table tool icon in the ToolBar.

❸ Drag the table grid that appears until the dimensions highlighted are the size for table you want to create.

❹ Release the mouse button.

You can expand a table at any time by selecting units of whatever you want to expand and clicking on the Table icon again. To select a row, put the cursor in the selection bar to the left of the table and click the left mouse button. To select a column, put the cursor at the top of any column and click the right mouse button. Next, click on the Table tool. An empty clone (row or column) of whatever you've selected will be inserted into the table either to the left of or immediately above the selected items.

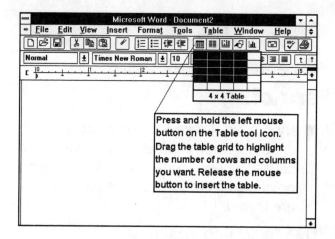

Press and hold the left mouse button on the Table tool icon. Drag the table grid to highlight the number of rows and columns you want. Release the mouse button to insert the table.

Create fixed line spacing

■ By default, *WinWord* bases line spacing on the tallest character in a line. This causes uneven formatting when varying point sizes, subscripts, and superscripts are mixed.

Use fixed line spacing.

❶ Move the insertion point (cursor) to the paragraph you want to format.

❷ Select Format Paragraph.

❸ Select Line Spacing (Alt-I).

❹ Select Exactly.

❺ Select At (Alt-A).

❻ Select a higher value than the one shown (by clicking the Up icon, by typing a number, or by pressing the Up key). If you are trying to uncramp superscripts and subscripts, creating fixed line spacing of 1.5 often does the trick. If you are trying to uncramp mixed fonts and even line spacing within a paragraph, enter the line spacing appropriate for the largest type size being used.

To even the line spacing in a paragraph that begins with an oversized initial capital letter, there is a better solution. Select Format Paragraph, as shown above, but set the Before spacing to a value large enough to accommo-

date the oversized capital letter. Then proceed
as shown, but set the fixed line spacing to that
required for the main text.

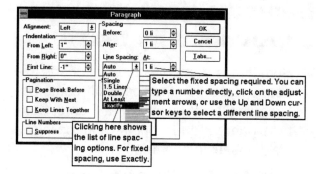

Evenly position a framed object that's surrounded by text

■ Sometimes framed pictures or charts appear offset rather than perfectly centered. Dragging the object, Format Frame, Center alignment, and cropping and scaling all yield unsatisfactory results.

Adjust the object's formatting.

The frame formatting inserted by *WinWord* is usually right on target, but you may need to adjust the object's paragraph formatting. If an object fails to center correctly, check the paragraph formatting. Make sure there is no automatic indentation that forces the object to the right, or line spacing that makes it appear too high or low.

❶ Position the insertion point in or on the object of interest. You need not select the whole item for paragraph formatting.

❷ Select Format Paragraph.

❸ If the item fails to center horizontally, verify that all three indentation values are 0.

❹ If the item fails to center vertically, verify that the Before and After spacing are identical.

You need not select Center alignment. When paragraph formatting is correctly set (no indentation and even before and after spacing), framing and positioning alone are sufficient for centering a framed object relative to surrounding text. If you want the object in the center of the page—rather than just evenly placed relative to the surrounding text—select Format Frame, and set the Horizontal Position to Center, relative to Margin, Page, or Column, whichever is relevant.

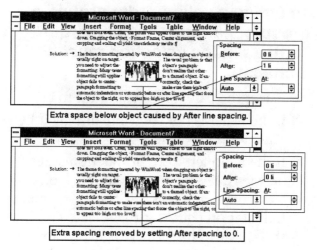

Extra space below object caused by After line spacing.

Extra spacing removed by setting After spacing to 0.

Build a border around several paragraphs

■ *WinWord* has built-in commands to put borders around single paragraphs, but not around a set of paragraphs.

To create a solid border around a group of paragraphs, all margin settings in the selection must be identical.

❶ Select the paragraphs you want to box.

❷ If the Ruler is not showing, display it by selecting View Ruler.

❸ If the main left or right indent markers on the Ruler are grayed out, click on the elements that are gray. This sets all main indentation equal for the selected text. If this disturbs the formatting, you can use first indents and tabs for horizontal placement.

❹ Select Format Border.

❺ Use the mouse to select your preferred border style.

❻ If you're boxing text, the default spacing of 1 point probably isn't enough. You will achieve better results with a separation of 5 to 10 points.

❼ Select View, Zoom, Whole Page.

❽ Select View, Page, Layout.

If you want to box an entire page, use the header procedure described in the *Microsoft*

Word User's Guide, "To place a border around every page in a section," (page 367 in the Version 2.0 guide).

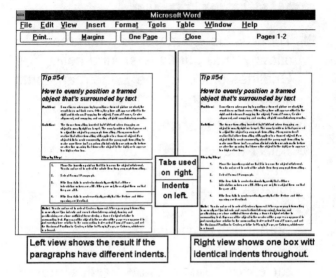

Left view shows the result if the paragraphs have different indents.

Right view shows one box with identical indents throughout.

Draw lines around the cells in a table

■ There is no Format Table command to allow you to put lines around cells. The Gridlines option on the Table menu puts lines on screen, not on paper.

Use Format Border.

❶ Select the whole table by pressing Alt-5 on the numeric keypad—Num Lock must be turned off.

❷ Select Format Border to activate the Border Table dialog box.

❸ If you want just an outside border around the entire table, with no interior lines, click in the area outside the table diagram in the Border area. Eight small triangles appear around the table diagram—two at each corner.

❹ Select a Line Style.

❺ If you want interior borders (horizontal, vertical, or both), click inside the Border table diagram until the corresponding lines are displayed.

❻ Select a Preset for Box or Shadow, whichever you prefer.

❼ Press Enter.

❽ If you want border variations for specific columns, rows, or cells, select only the portion you want to affect before selecting the Format Border dialog box. This will produce the Border Cells dialog box.

❾ While the Format Border dialog box is on-screen, you can alternately click on the Border diagram and Line selection box to turn various border components on and off.

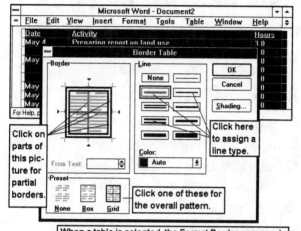

When a table is selected, the Format Border command produces a Border Table dialog box. If just part of the table is selected, you'll get the Border Cells dialog box.

Place legal-style line numbers along the left-hand side of the page

■ Briefing papers, contracts, depositions, and other legal documents require line numbers in some states.

Use Format Section Layout.

❶ Select Format Section Layout.

❷ Select Line Numbers.

❸ Select Add Line Numbering; click so that an X appears in the checkbox.

❹ Set Start at to 1.

❺ Set Count by to 1.

❻ Set Distance from text to .5".

❼ Set Restart at to every new page.

❽ Click on OK (to close the Line Number dialog box).

❾ Click on OK (to close the Format Section Layout dialog box).

For uniform spacing of line numbers, you also must select exact or fixed line spacing. Typical legal style uses 10 point type size with 12 point spacing (6 lines per inch). Furthermore, all line spacing must be accomplished with actual lines of text or carriage returns—not with before and after paragraph spacing. Line numbers will not be printed in spaces forced down by other formatting methods. Finally, line numbers display only in print preview and when printed.

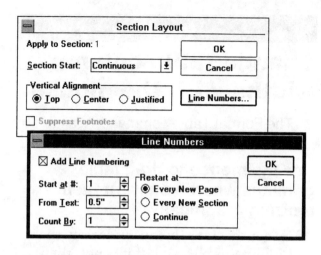

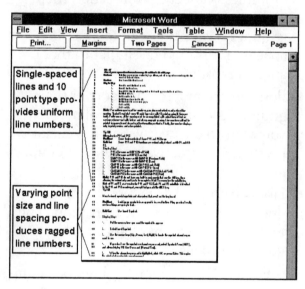

Single-spaced lines and 10 point type provides uniform line numbers.

Varying point size and line spacing produces ragged line numbers.

Change table column widths with the mouse

■ The Format Table command, available in *WinWord* 1, is missing from version 2.

Use the mouse to drag table gridlines where you want them, resizing graphically.

❶ Select the Table menu, and verify that Gridlines is checked. If it is not, then highlight it and press Enter. With gridlines turned on, your table's appearance should be similar to that of an Excel worksheet matrix.

❷ Position the mouse pointer over the gridline associated with the dimension you want to change. When the cursor is positioned correctly, it assumes a double arrow shape.

❸ Hold down the left mouse button and drag the gridline to a new position. The table column widths change as the gridline is dragged.

Most Format Table commands have been simplified by providing a mouse alternative. If you prefer the precision of a menu, however, column widths are now under Table Column Width; rows are under Table Row Height; and cell lines are under Format Border. Other table features are also provided in the Table menu.

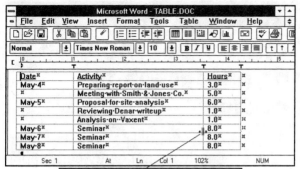

Date	Activity	Hours
Date¤	Activity¤	Hours¤ ¤
May·4¤	Preparing·report·on·land·use¤	3.0¤ ¤
¤	Meeting·with·Smith·&·Jones·Co.¤	5.0¤ ¤
May·5¤	Proposal·for·site·analysis¤	6.0¤ ¤
¤	Reviewing·Denar·writeup¤	1.0¤ ¤
¤	Analysis·on··Vaxent¤	1.0¤ ¤
May·6¤	Seminar¤	8.0¤ ¤
May·7¤	Seminar¤	8.0¤ ¤
May·8¤	Seminar¤	8.0¤ ¤

Use the ◄‖► to adjust column width. Unlike
The T on the Ruler, the ◄‖► changes the width
of the entire column, without selection, not
just the width of a single cell.

Tip #48

Copy formatting from one paragraph to another

■ It's tedious to reformat paragraphs manually, especially when nearby paragraphs already contain the necessary formatting. It's especially aggravating when the formatting you want is a style variation, rather than something you could accomplish just by applying another style.

Copy only the paragraph mark.

❶ Make certain that paragraph markers are visible. If they are not, press Ctrl-Shift-8 on the number pad to toggle them on.

❷ Select the paragraph mark of the paragraph whose formatting you want to copy.

❸ Press Shift-F2.

❹ Select the paragraph mark of the paragraph you want to reformat. Notice that the selection is highlighted with a dotted line instead of reverse video. This is a characteristic of the CopyText command (Shift-F2).

❺ Press Enter. This copies the formatting to the paragraph.

If you want to copy the format to more than one paragraph, in step 2, press Ctrl-Insert instead of Shift-F2. Then select the paragraph marker of each paragraph you want to reformat and press Shift-Insert.

Invoke Format Styles using a keystroke

■ Selecting Format Styles using the menu (Alt-T Y) is an unintuitive combination: T for format? Y for style?

Press Ctrl-S—twice.

❶ Put the cursor in the paragraph you want to affect.

❷ Press Ctrl-S twice. The first Ctrl-S gets the *Which Style?* question (or the drop down list box in the ribbon). The second Ctrl-S gets the Format Styles dialog box.

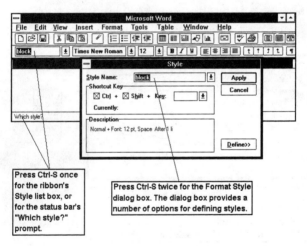

Press Ctrl-S once for the ribbon's Style list box, or for the status bar's "Which style?" prompt.

Press Ctrl-S twice for the Format Style dialog box. The dialog box provides a number of options for defining styles.

Make quick changes to a style using shortcut keys

■ Selecting Format Styles Define, and then having to select each of its different aspects, is time consuming.

Use shortcut formatting keys in the Format Styles dialog box.

❶ Position the cursor in the paragraph you want to affect.

❷ Press Ctrl-S, twice.

❸ Select the style you want to edit.

❹ Use formatting keys to display or turn off formatting in the Description area.

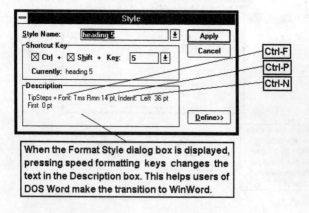

When the Format Style dialog box is displayed, pressing speed formatting keys changes the text in the Description box. This helps users of DOS Word make the transition to WinWord.

Keys used to change format

Style	Description
Ctrl-O	Add line spacing before paragraph
Ctrl-A	All capital letters
Ctrl-B	Bold
Ctrl-E	Centered paragraph
Ctrl-0	Delete line spacing before paragraph
Ctrl-D	Double underline
Ctrl-2	Double-spaced lines
Ctrl-F	Font
Ctrl-T	Hanging indent
Ctrl-H	Hidden text
Ctrl-P	Increase point size
Ctrl-N	Indent paragraph
Ctrl-I	Italic
Ctrl-J	Justified paragraph
Ctrl-L	Left-aligned paragraph
Ctrl-5	One-and-one-half-spaced lines
Ctrl-G	Reduce hanging indent
Ctrl-M	Reduce left indent
Ctrl-Space	Remove all variant character formatting (except font)
Ctrl-Q	Remove all variant paragraph formatting
Ctrl-R	Right-aligned paragraph
Ctrl-1	Single-spaced lines
Ctrl-K	Small capital letters
Ctrl-=	Subscript (3 points)
Ctrl-Shift-=	Superscript (3 points)
Ctrl-U	Underline
Ctrl-W	Word underline

Show all built-in or standard styles

■ *WinWord* has 34 standard or built-in styles, but they only appear when you use a related feature.

Press Ctrl-Y in the Format Styles dialog box.

❶ Select Format Styles (shortcut: press Ctrl-S twice).

❷ Press Alt-Down (this expands the list box to show a list of styles).

❸ Press Ctrl-Y to toggle the list of standard styles on and off. Once displayed, these styles may be selected and applied normally.

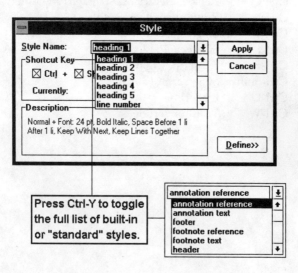

Press Ctrl-Y to toggle the full list of built-in or "standard" styles.

The Standard Styles

annotation reference
annotation text
footer
footnote reference
footnote text
header
heading 1
heading 2
heading 3
heading 4
heading 5
heading 6
heading 7
heading 8
heading 9
index 1
index 2
index 3
index 4
index 5
index 6
index 7
index heading
line number
Normal
Normal Indent
toc 1
toc 2
toc 3
toc 4
toc 5
toc 6
toc 7
toc 8

Copy all style changes to a template

■ Selecting Format Styles Define, an inefficient way to format a document, appears to be the only way to modify styles in a template.

Use Format Styles Define Merge to copy all styles to or from a template.

❶ Select Format Style (Ctrl-S twice).

❷ Select Define (Alt-D).

❸ Select Merge (Alt-M).

❹ Select the template you want to change.

❺ Select To Template (Alt-P).

❻ If the current document contains styles with identical names as those in the receiving template, you will be prompted *Merging will replace the styles in (filename) with new styles of the same name. Do you want to replace the styles?* Select Yes to complete the merge.

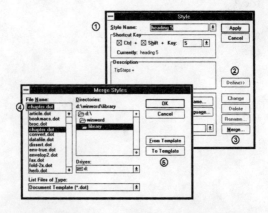

Toggle character formatting on and off

■ Selecting Format Character is a difficult way to apply character attributes such as bold or italic.

Use speed formatting keys.

❶ When you come to a section you want to make bold, press Ctrl-B.

❷ Type your text.

❸ Press Ctrl-B to turn bold formatting off.

❹ Resume typing.

The identical technique can be used with each of the shortcuts shown in Tip #34. In addition, Ctrl-Space can be used to remove *all* character formatting that varies from the underlying style. But, Ctrl-Space is not necessarily a way to turn off character formatting. For example, if you enter text in a section that you have already made bold, and press Ctrl-I, you get Bold Italic. If you press Ctrl-I again to turn off italic, you resume bold typing. However if you press Ctrl-Space, you turn off both bold and italic, which may not be what you intend.

Strip all formatting from a document quickly and easily

■ Sometimes you must completely remove all formatting from a document, and plodding through each option under Format Character and Format Paragraph seems like too much work.

Use ResetPara and ResetChar.

❶ Press Ctrl-5, on the number pad, to select the entire document.

❷ Press Ctrl-Space to remove all variant character formatting.

❸ Press Ctrl-Q to format all paragraphs the same as the first paragraph in the selection. This assigns the first style encountered to all paragraphs and removes all variant paragraph formatting. Alternatively, perform Tip #55.

❹ To assign the Normal style to all paragraphs in the selection, press Alt-Shift-5 (numeric keypad, Num Lock off).

Shortcut for assigning the Normal style to a paragraph

■ Pressing Ctrl-S and selecting Normal from a list wears thin if you change styles a lot.

Use the built-in shortcut.

❶ Put the insertion point anywhere in the paragraph you want to format.

❷ Press Alt-Shift-5 on the numeric keypad (Num Lock must be off).

You can automate style selection somewhat by setting the Format Styles Define Next Style as Normal wherever appropriate. For example, set the Next Style as Normal for Heading styles that are always followed by Normal text. Each time you press Enter after typing a heading, the style of the next paragraph automatically becomes Normal.

Determine whether character formatting in a selection is identical

■ You often need to determine whether a section of a document contains any formatting differences.

Select the section, and then use a Format Character dialog box.

❶ Select the text of interest.

❷ Press Ctrl-F, twice.

❸ Look at the format settings. Any that are selected or completely unselected are consistent throughout the selection. Any that are "grayed out," or which don't display a setting value, indicate that the selection contains at least two different settings for that formatting type. For example, if the Bold checkbox is grayed out, rather than white or marked with an "X," then the selection contains a mixture of text that is bold and not bold. If the Font name is not displayed, then the selection contains at least two different fonts.

If you select more than 50 paragraphs (any combination of more than 50 page elements), this technique does not work. If the selection appears to be completely mixed for all formatting types, it is likely that more than 50 page elements are selected. Reduce the size of the selection and try again. Page elements include paragraph markers, table cell markers, section breaks, column breaks, and page breaks. In a 10 × 6 table, for example, all formatting attributes will appear to be ambiguous, even when they are absolutely identical.

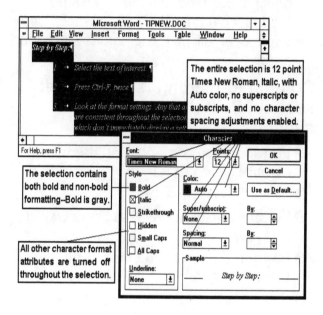

Center a title over a multi-column page

■ When you use Format Column to create multiple columns, the title shows up over the first column. Ideally, you want it centered over all of the columns—not just one.

Column formatting is applied per section. Split the page into two sections.

❶ Position the insertion point after the carriage return that follows the title.

❷ Select Insert Break (Alt-I B).

❸ Select Continuous section break (Alt-T) and press Enter.

❹ Position the insertion point in the same line as the title.

❺ Select Format Columns (Alt-T O).

❻ If the section is formatted for more than one column, use the Down arrow to reduce the number of columns to 1 and press Enter.

❼ Move the insertion point to the beginning of the text you want in columns.

❽ Select Format Columns.

❾ If the section currently is not formatted for the number of columns you want, use the Up arrow key to increase the number of columns you want. Select any other relevant options at this time, also.

❿ Press Enter.

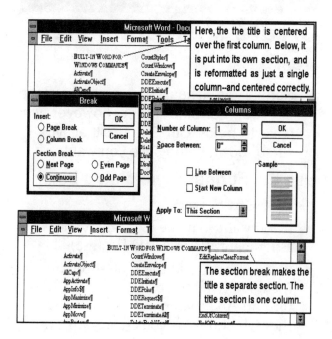

Here, the the title is centered over the first column. Below, it is put into its own section, and is reformatted as just a single column--and centered correctly.

The section break makes the title a separate section. The title section is one column.

Create shortcut style keys

■ Normal format has a built-in shortcut (see Tip #55). For other styles, however, you have to press Ctrl-S and either type or cursor-down to the style you want.

Use the Format Style dialog box.

❶ Press Ctrl-S, twice.

❷ If you want to make more than one assignment, Press Alt-D (Define)

❸ If you want to add the style shortcuts to the underlying template, press Alt-E to turn on Add to Template. Otherwise, the style shortcuts you create will exist only in the current document.

❹ Select the style for which you want to create a shortcut (Alt-S).

❺ Select the key you want to use (Alt-Y).

❻ Select Change (Alt-A).

❼ Repeat Steps 4 through 6 until you have assigned as many styles as you want.

❽ Select Close.

❾ When you exit from *WinWord*, say Yes to the prompt *Save global glossary and command changes* or *Save changes to [template].DOT* (where [template] is the actual template name). Alternatively, you can select File Save All (Alt-F E) now and answer Yes to the appropriate Save prompts.

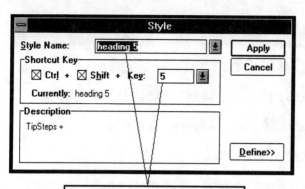

Above, the "heading 5" style is given the shortcut Ctrl-Shift-5.

Call the character formatting dialog box with a keyboard shortcut

■ Pressing Alt-T C for character formatting is not intuitive, nor is it especially easy.

Use Ctrl-F or Ctrl-P.

● Press either Ctrl-F or Ctrl-P, twice.

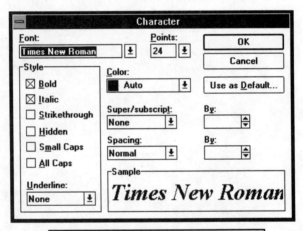

Press either Ctrl-F or Ctrl-P twice for the Format Character dialog box

Move a frame with the mouse

■ Using Format Frame to position a framed object or text is unintuitive and difficult.

Use the mouse.

❶ Select View Page Layout.

❷ Click the mouse left button on text outside the framed object.

❸ Move the mouse pointer over the framed object without clicking. As you do, a crossed arrow pointer will appear.

❹ To move the whole framed area, drag it to its destination. To drag it, hold down the left mouse button and move the frame outline to a new location. When you release the mouse button, *WinWord* adjusts the display to reflect the new location, and displays eight sizing handles.

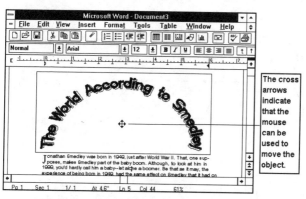

The cross arrows indicate that the mouse can be used to move the object.

Hold down the left mouse button, and the move the mouse until the object is positioned as you like it.

Restore *Word for Windows* to a partial window in just two steps

■ Restoring *WinWord* to a partial window that can be resized is a multi-step process if you use the menu.

Double-click anywhere in the Microsoft Word title bar.

❶ Put the mouse pointer anywhere in the Microsoft Word title bar.

❷ Double-click the mouse left button. Repeatedly double-clicking toggles the window between maximized and restored states.

A Windows application can exist in three states: Maximized (occupies the whole window and can't be resized using the mouse); Minimized (seen only as an icon); and Normal (also called Restored, this is a partial window that can be resized using the mouse).

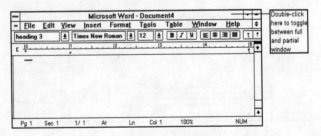

Double-click here to toggle between full and partial window

Maximize a window with the title bar

■ It takes pin-point precision (and too much time) to aim the mouse at the document maximize button.

Double-click anywhere in the document title bar.

❶ Position the mouse anywhere in the document title bar.

❷ Double-click.

When maximized, the document title and the Microsoft Word title both are displayed in the application title bar area. When a document is in a partial window, it has a separate title bar. Contrast the views shown in Tips #61 and #62. In Tip #61, the Microsoft Word and Document 4 title bars are merged at the top of the window. In Tip #62, Microsoft Word and Document 4 are shown with distinct title bars because Document 4 is not maximized.

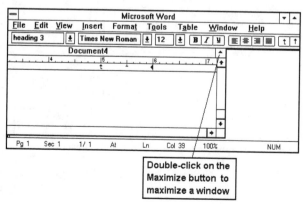

Double-click on the Maximize button to maximize a window

Restore and size the *WinWord* window at the same time

■ If you want to go from a full-screen to a window size other than the current one, you must first click on the restore button and then manipulate the window borders.

Use the sizing drag box.

❶ Position the mouse on the drag box, as shown.

❷ Press the left mouse button, and drag the lower right corner of the window until *WinWord* is the size and shape you want. Vertical and horizontal dimensions change at the same time.

The sizing drag box works with both a maximized and a restored window, and is much easier to manipulate than the absolute left corner (which produces a diagonal sizing arrow).

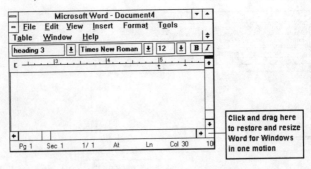

Click and drag here to restore and resize Word for Windows in one motion

View the whole document width regardless of screen resolution

■ In standard VGA resolution (640 x 480), only about 6.5 inches of document width can be seen.

Use ViewZoomPageWidth.

❶ Click on the ViewZoomPageWidth icon in the ToolBar. This corresponds to the View Zoom PageWidth command in the View Zoom dialog box. This command automatically scales the zoom/ magnification so that the whole width of the page is visible.

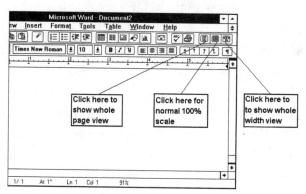

Show the style name without using the Ribbon.

■ When the Ribbon isn't showing, for example when a macro editing pane is active, it's difficult to determine what style is in use.

Turn on the style area.

❶ Select Tools Options View (Alt-O O V).

❷ Press Alt-W to go to the Style Area Width text box.

❸ If your style names tend to be fairly short (fewer than 8 characters), type **.5"**, or use the mouse to click the dimension control up arrow until the text box reads .5". Select a slightly larger value if your style names tend to be long.

❹ Press Enter or select the OK button.

When you return to your document, the left side of your screen will display the style associated with each paragraph. Note that unlike many *WinWord* procedures, there is no short-cut for displaying the style area. Once it's displayed, however, you can use the mouse to resize it or hide it. Once hidden, though, you must use Tools Options View to show it again.

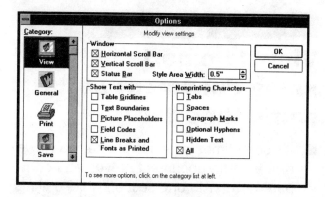

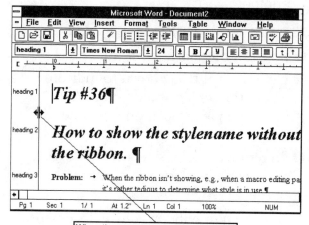

When the mouse cursor is on the style bar, it takes the shape of a sizing arrow

View two parts of the same document at the same time

■ It's sometimes useful to create two views of the same document so you can compare or refer to one section while editing another.

Use the Split Box.

❶ Position the mouse over the Split Box.

❷ Drag the Split Box down to indicate where the screen should split. You now have two panes open on the same document.

❸ To remove a split, select the Split Box and drag it as close as you can to the top of the screen.

Having a split window on a document is different than having two windows open on the same document. In both cases, all views of the identical document are updated simultaneously whenever you add, move, delete, or change anything. When you use the Split box, a second *pane* is opened—both panes occupying a single *WinWord* window. When you use Alt-W N, however, *WinWord* actually opens a second *window* on the same document. You can close a second *pane* by dragging the Split Box to the top of the screen. You close a second *window* by pressing Ctrl-F4.

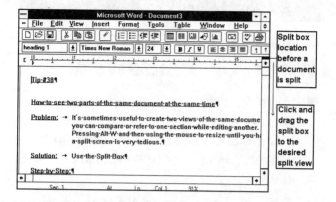

Split box
location
before a
document
is split

Click and
drag the
split box
to the
desired
split view

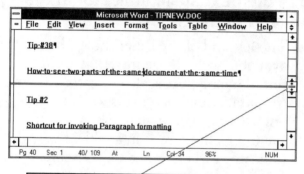

When the mouse pointer is over the split box, it becomes
a sizing arrow that can be dragged to split the document.

Change Ruler views in *Word for Windows 2*

■ *Word for Windows* 1 had a ruler icon to change Ruler scales among paragraph, margin, and table view. It's missing from version 2. How do you change Ruler scales in version 2?

Use the next scale indicator at the left end of the Ruler.

❶ The left end of the Ruler shows the next available scale. If the insertion point is not in a table, the scale indicator will be [(margin view) or a two-segment right-pointing triangle (paragraph view). If the insertion point is in a table, the scale indicator will also offer a T for table view.

❷ Click on the [, triangle, or T icons to switch into the next available view.

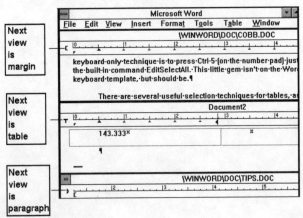

Set View Preferences

■ *WinWord* 1 had a menu item called View Preferences. There is no such selection in *WinWord* 2

It moved to the Tools Options menu.

❶ Select Tools Options View (Alt-O O V).

❷ Select your options from those shown.

❸ Press Enter. Options you select are retained during the current session, and are preserved in WINWORD.INI when you close *Word for Windows*.

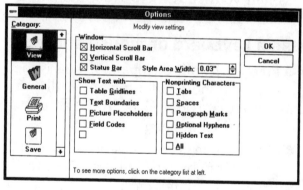

Toggle the display of paragraph markers, spaces, and other special symbols

■ Many tasks can be clarified if you can see paragraph markers, tabs, spaces, and other nonprinting characters on screen. On the other hand, if you want to see how the document will look on paper, you don't want the nonprinting characters on screen. If you toggle nonprinting character display often, you need a more direct method than the Tools Options View approach.

Use a keyboard or mouse shortcut.

● Press Ctrl-Shift-8 (top row). This is the keyboard shortcut for the ShowAll toggle that is embedded in the Tools Options View menu.

● If the ribbon is On, click on the ¶ icon at the far right end. This replaces the * icon used in *WinWord* 1.1.

Because of a bug in early versions of *WinWord* 2, Ctrl-* (on the number pad), does not work, despite its being documented on the keyboard template and other *WinWord* materials. Those used to using Ctrl-* from the program's version 1 may wish to use Tools Options Keyboard to assign the ShowAll command to Ctrl-* on the number pad.

Print an envelope without using templates

■ Using the envelope templates seems needlessly complex.

Use the ToolsCreateEnvelope command.

❶ Select the address you want printed on the envelope. In some cases, *WinWord* can find the TO address on its own, but preselecting is a safer bet.

❷ Click on the Envelope Icon.

❸ If you want to print the envelope immediately, fill in your return address (if necessary—see Tools Options User Info, Alt-O O U to permanently set your return address) and press Enter.

❹ If you want to make the envelope part of the current document, then select that option (Alt-A). This creates an envelope section at the beginning of your document, with a section break between the envelope and the rest of the document. The envelope will print along with your document.

The envelope command cannot locate the address automatically if it contains new line separators (Shift-Enter) instead of paragraph breaks (Enter). Beware of this anomaly when using documents created in earlier versions of *Word for Windows*.

Print a document from back to front

■ When using a laser printer's *straight-through* path for labels and other specialty papers, the document pages end up stacked last-to-first and have to be reordered.

Tell *WinWord* to reverse-order print.

❶ Select Tools Options Print (Alt-O O P).

❷ Select Options (Alt-O).

❸ From the Options menu, select **Reverse Print Order** (Alt-R) so that the box is checked with an X.

❹ Press Enter.

This option can be selected from the File Print Options menu or from the Tools Options Print menu. In either case, this selection remains in effect until you turn it off. Like many Tools Options settings, Reverse Print Order is an assignable default that is retained in WINWORD.INI between sessions.

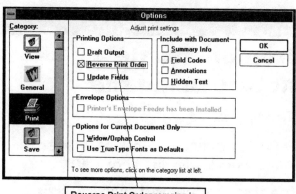

Reverse Print Order remains in
effect until you de-select it from
the Options Print dialog box.

Crop and scale a picture using the mouse

■ Setting picture dimensions by specifying numbers is trial and error.

Use the mouse and picture sizing handles.

❶ Select Normal View (Alt-V N) if you're not already there.

❷ Click the mouse left button anywhere on the picture. This causes eight sizing handles to appear around the picture.

❸ To scale, drag any of the eight sizing handles to a location that makes the picture the size you want. You can drag the sizing handles by putting the mouse cursor over any of the eight boxes, and then holding down the left mouse button while you move the mouse. Note that the sizing handles move as the mouse moves.

❹ To crop, use the same technique as in Step 3, but press Shift while holding the left mouse button and moving the mouse.

Cropping removes part of the picture from the top, bottom, or sides, while scaling increases or decreases the size of the entire picture.

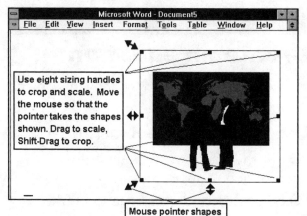

Use eight sizing handles to crop and scale. Move the mouse so that the pointer takes the shapes shown. Drag to scale, Shift-Drag to crop.

Mouse pointer shapes indicate the directions of size/scale changes.

Create an equation

■ *WinWord*'s equation editor isn't on the menu.

Use the Insert Object menu.

❶ Put the cursor where you want the equation to appear.

❷ Select Insert Object Equation (Alt-I O E).

❸ Use the equation editor to create the equation you desire.

❹ When you're finished creating the equation, select File Close, and the equation editor will ask if you want to save the equation to your *WinWord* document. If you say yes, then the equation will be preserved as an {EMBED Equation} field.

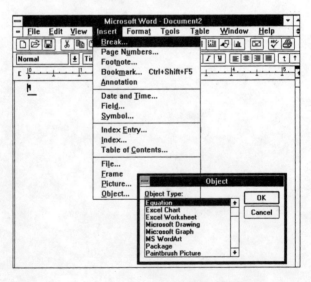

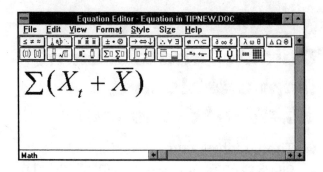

Quickly create a chart from a table in a *WinWord* document

■ The Graph feature is useful, but it's tedious to enter the data or to try to import it.

***WinWord* can automatically import data from a table when you select the Graph feature.**

❶ Position the insertion point (cursor) in the table.

❷ If Num Lock is on, press the Num Lock key to turn it off.

❸ Press Alt-5 on the numeric keypad to select the entire table.

❹ Click on the Graph icon in the ToolBar, or select Insert Object Microsoft Graph. The hourglass appears as Microsoft Graph imports the data from the table.

The upper left cell is used for the graph's main title. Note also that years in the table had to be enclosed in quotes. Otherwise, Microsoft Graph would have registered the years as data points, the scale of which overwhelms the actual data points. If the years had been text instead of numbers, no quotes would have been needed.

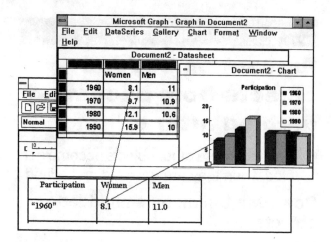

Participation	Women	Men
"1960"	8.1	11.0

Prevent embedded objects from becoming garbled after editing

■ Equations and other objects become garbled when they are unlinked and edited.

Don't use Unlink on embedded objects.

When you use the equation editor to create an equation, you can only re-edit that equation using the equation editor if the {EMBED equation} field remains a field. Once you press Ctrl-Shift-F9 to unlink the object, *WinWord* no longer knows it is an equation. When you click on the resulting graphic to edit it, *WinWord* uses MS Draw instead of the equation editor.

Objects are specific to the application that created them. Only objects created with MS Draw can be unlinked safely, since MS Draw is the default editor used when you edit pictures contained (not embedded) in a Word document.

Objects created using the equation editor, MS Graph, MS Excel, or other applications should be maintained as objects if you want to preserve the ability to edit them at a later time.

Select dialog box options using the keyboard

■ Tabbing to option buttons and using the mouse disrupts keyboard-oriented users.

Use the accelerator keys.

❶ Select Format Paragraph (Alt-T P).

❷ Note that each keyword contains an underlined letter: Alignment, From Left, From Right, First Line. In each case, you can move the cursor directly to the keyword by typing Alt plus the underlined letter. Alt-G for Alignment, Alt-L for From Left, Alt-R for From Right, and Alt-F for First Line. Because each accelerator character must be unique, some unlikely letters are underlined.

The Alt-*letter* paradigm is an aspect of the CUA interface characteristic of Windows and OS/2 Presentation Manager (see Tip #5).

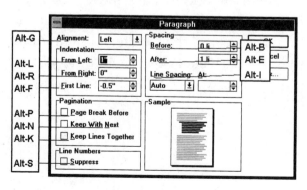

Discover a key's purpose

■ If you know a command or procedure name, you usually can find out what key to press. But, how do you find out what any given key does?

Use the Tools Options Keys menu.

❶ Select the Tools Options Keyboard menu (press Alt-O O K).

❷ If it does not involve an Alt key, press the key combination of interest. For example, press Ctrl-N. *WinWord* displays the associated command (if any).

❸ If the key combination involves the Alt key, or otherwise doesn't seem to "register," you can peruse the list of assigned keys for commands or macros, along with the corresponding global or template context.

The Alt keys don't work in step two because *WinWord* responds to them rather than reveals their functions. Thus, if you press Alt-O from within the keyboard options menu, *WinWord* selects the Command item, rather than reveals what Alt-O might otherwise do. (Alt-O usually selects the Tools menu).

When you press a key combination, the key and command become highlighted in the Shortcut Key Group, as well as in the commands group.

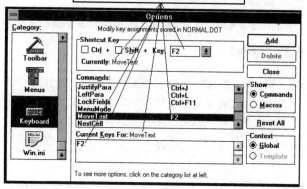

To see more options, click on the category list at left.

Toggle between *WinWord* and the Help screen

■ When you invoke Help, it can be tedious to get back to the *WinWord* screen. The problem is exacerbated when you want to retain the Help screen information to refer to it.

Use Alt-Tab to toggle between Help and *WinWord*.

❶ Press F1 for Help. Navigate the Help menu to find the information you need.

❷ When you're ready, press Alt-Tab to go back to *WinWord*.

❸ To return to the help screen, press Alt-Tab again.

When you hold the Alt key and press Tab successively, Windows steps through all active applications. However, if you remove your finger from the Alt key after a press of Alt-Tab, Alt-Tab serves as a toggle between the two most recently accessed applications. This technique works for any two applications that are conceptually adjacent—that is, the last two accessed.

Adjust numbers in a text box

■ It would be nice to be able to change format dimensions without retyping.

Use the adjustment arrows.

❶ Select Format Paragraph, for example. The insertion point will be in the Left Indentation text box.

❷ Either: 1) Click on the up or down adjustment arrows to increase or decrease the value of the indentation; or 2) Use the Up or Down cursor keys to perform the same adjustment. If you hold down the mouse button or cursor keys, the value in the text box will change rapidly after a second or so.

Adjustment arrows work in a variety of dialog boxes—Format Paragraph, Insert Table, View Zoom. Anywhere you see the adjustment arrows, you can use the mouse or cursor keys to increase or decrease the values.

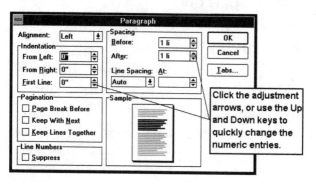

Click the adjustment arrows, or use the Up and Down keys to quickly change the numeric entries.

Alternates for F11 and F12

■ Some keyboards don't have F11 and F12 keys.

Some F11 and F12 functions are redundantly defined as Alt-F1 and Alt-F2.

● F11 is the same as Alt-F1 (Next Field).

● F12 is the same as Alt-F2 (Save As).

● Shift-F11 is the same as Alt-Shift-F11 (Previous Field).

● Shift-F12 is the same as Alt-Shift-F12 (Save).

● Ctrl-F11 is the same as Alt-Ctrl-F11 (Lock Field).

● Ctrl-F12 is the same as Alt-Ctrl-F12 (File Open).

● Ctrl-Shift-F11 is the same as Alt-Ctrl-Shift-F11 (Unlock Field).

● Ctrl-Shift-F12 is the same as Alt-Ctrl-Shift-F12 (Print).

F11 and F12 have no built-in assignments that use the Alt key.

Hint: To remember the substitutes, think of F1 and F2 as *alt*ernates for F11 and F12. Each F1 and F2 substitute is identical to its F11 and F12 counterpart, except that you add the **ALT** key.

Close only the current window or pane

■ Users often accidentally close *WinWord* when trying to close a document.

Understand and use control icons.

● To close a pane, click on the Close button (or press Alt-Shift-C).

● To close a document window or a macro window, double-click the document control icon (Ctrl-F4). If more than one view of that document is open, this action closes only the current view.

● To close all views of a file, select File Close (Alt-F C).

● To close *WinWord*, double-click on the application control icon (Alt-F4).

● To close Windows, double-click on the Program Manager's application control icon.

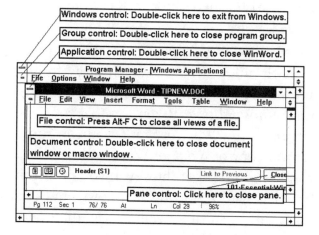

Escape from *WinWord's* hourglass

■ During field updates in a large document, and when printing, *WinWord* can display its hourglass for what seems like hours.

Restore before running.

❶ If *WinWord* is maximized, click on the Restore button before starting the time-consuming procedure.

❷ Start the procedure—Print, Update Fields, Sort, Mail Merge.

❸ Move the hourglass so that it is over the program manager (in the background window) and click. The focus shifts away from *WinWord*, and the task runs in the background.

Even though the cursor is an hourglass shape, which usually means "wait," you *can* switch to another application—if another application is visible on your desktop. If *WinWord* is max-imized, however, you must wait for the hour-glass to disappear before you can switch away.

This tip allows you to switch away from a *WinWord* print job and continue working on a non-*WinWord* task. If you want to continue working on a *WinWord* task, you can run a second copy of *Word for Windows* in another window. To do that, however, you must run SHARE before starting Windows, and you must have sufficient memory installed.

SHARE.EXE is a DOS utility that, among other things, prevents files from being written to simultaneously by multiple programs. See your DOS manual for more information.

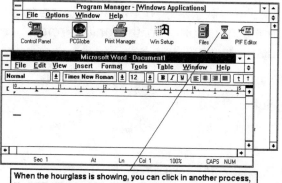

When the hourglass is showing, you can click in another process, like the Program Manager, to switch away from Word for Windows. To switch, WinWord can't be maximized -- it must be in a window.

Get syntax help for macro commands

■ Looking up macro commands in the reference manual or in the online reference disrupts work flow.

Press F1 while editing a macro.

❶ Select Tools Macro.

❷ Select a macro to edit.

❸ Press Alt-E.

❹ Position the cursor on any macro command name and press F1. *WinWord*'s help system will show you the syntax and usage of the command. You can then use Alt-Tab to toggle between the help screen and the macro—see Tip #78.

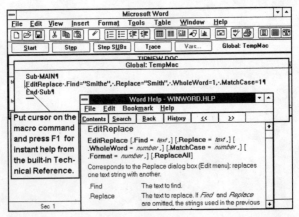

Copy Help information to the Clipboard

■ Sometimes you might want to copy Help information so you can refer to it without having to renavigate the menu.

Copy it to the Clipboard, and then into a document.

❶ Press F1.

❷ Find the Help item of interest.

❸ Press Ctrl-Insert. This copies the entire scrollable area (text only) of the Help screen to the Clipboard.

❹ Press Alt-F4 to close Help, or Alt-Tab to switch away from Help back to *WinWord*.

❺ Position the cursor in the document where you want to copy the help information.

❻ Press Shift-Insert.

Some possible uses for this procedure include making a reference sheet for a difficult procedure, listing keyboard or mouse shortcuts, and detailing field switches or options. However, if there are deeply embedded Help topics you refer to often, don't overlook the Help bookmark feature.

Create expandable abbreviations and shorthands

■ When typing text, it's tedious to repeatedly retype commonly used phrases such as Microsoft *Word for Windows*, the *American Journal of Pyrotechnics*, or multiple personality disorder.

Create shorthands and abbreviations with the glossary.

❶ Type and format a word or phrase exactly as you want it inserted in the text.

❷ Select the entire word or phrase.

❸ Select Edit Glossary, from the menu.

❹ Type a short abbreviation for the phrase. For example, you could use **msww** for Microsoft *Word for Windows*. For the *American Journal of Psychology*, you might use **ajp**. (Remember to format *American Journal of Psychology* as italic, if that's the way it normally would appear in your text.)

❺ The next time you need to insert the glossary item, just type the abbreviation and press F3.

Glossary names (the abbreviations you use) can be up to 31 characters, but if they are that long, they're hardly shorthand, anymore. Glossary names can include any characters you

like, but are not case-specific. Hence, AJP and
ajp are identical.

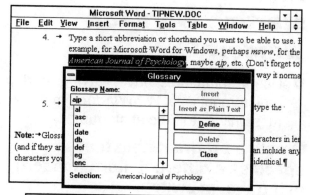

Microsoft Word - TIPNEW.DOC							▼ ▲
<u>F</u>ile	<u>E</u>dit	<u>V</u>iew	<u>I</u>nsert	For<u>m</u>at	T<u>o</u>ols	T<u>a</u>ble	<u>W</u>indow	<u>H</u>elp ♦

4. → Type a short abbreviation or shorthand you want to be able to use. F
example, for Microsoft Word for Windows, perhaps *msww*, for the
American Journal of Psychology, maybe *ajp*, etc. (Don't forget to way it norma

Glossary

Glossary **N**ame:

ajp

al
asc
cr
date
db
def
eg
enc

Insert

Insert as Plain Text

Define

Delete

Close

type the

Selection: American Journal of Psychology

Note: → Gloss characters in let
(and if they ar an include any
characters you identical. ¶

Once ajp is defined as a glossary name for the selection, you can type
ajp, press F3, and it will expand into *American Journal of Psychology*.

Run a macro when starting *Word for Windows*

■ Users sometimes have varying startup requirements, but *WinWord* automatically runs only AutoExec at startup.

Create a program item that specifies a different startup macro using the /m switch.

❶ From the Windows Program Manager, select File New, Program Item, and then click on OK.

❷ Select any appropriate description, working directory, and shortcut key you want to associate with the new item.

❸ Under **Command Line**, type:

winword /m*macro*

where *macro* is the name of the macro you want *WinWord* to use at startup. For example, if you want *WinWord* to automatically load the last file you edited, specify:

winword /mfile1.

with no spaces between /, m, or file1. To have *WinWord* automatically run a macro called LetterSetup, specify:

winword /mlettersetup.

❹ Select OK to save the new program item. Make sure that you save your Windows settings when you exit from

Windows. Using this new program item, you will be able to launch an alternative version of *WinWord*.

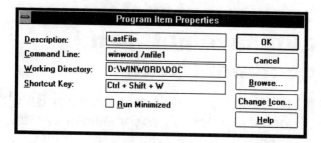

Change the default backup extension, autosave path, and document path

■ *WinWord* uses a default extension of .BAK for backup files. Users sometimes want to specify their own extension and paths.

Change the BAK-EXTENSION setting (and others) in WIN.INI.

❶ Select Tools Options WIN.INI (Alt-O O W).

❷ Under Options, type **BAK-EXTENSION**.

❸ Under Setting, type the extension you prefer, for example, **.BWK** (including the period).

❹ Select the Set option, and then the Close option.

Several options can be set using this technique:

    TOOLS-PATH
    INI-PATH
    DOT-PATH
    AUTOSAVE-PATH
    DOC-PATH
    TIMEFORMAT
    DATEFORMAT
    CONVERSION
    DRAWAPPNAME
    NOVELLNET
    SLOWSHADING
    NOFILECACHE

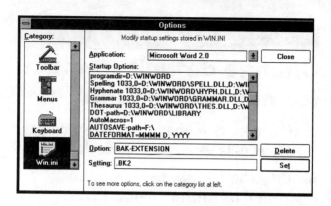

Change default format for new documents

■ The default format (font, size) for new documents usually is unacceptable.

Modify the template using the Format Character dialog box.

❶ Select File New.

❷ In the *Use Template* box, select the template whose default font you want to change.

❸ Select Format Character (Ctrl-F twice).

❹ Use the Format Character controls to set the font you want.

❺ Click on *Use as Default*.

❻ You will be prompted *Do you want to change the font for the Normal style to. . .* The prompt may further remind you that the change will affect all documents based on that template. Click on **Yes**.

❼ When you Exit from *Word for Windows*, you will see a prompt such as: *Do you want to save global command and glossary changes?* You must answer **Yes** to this prompt in order to make the change permanent.

This procedure differs markedly from that required by *Word for Windows* 1.

Shortcut for invoking Tools Options ToolBar

■ Pressing Alt-O O T isn't quick and intuitive (How could Alt-O for Tool be intuitive?), nor is making the comparable selection with a mouse.

Use the ToolBar itself.

● Double-click on any blank area in the ToolBar.

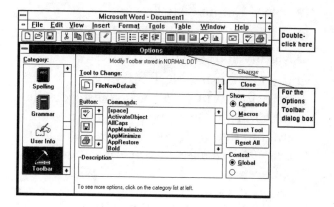

Add style changes to the template

■ When users make changes to the document, macros, and glossary, *WinWord* prompts *Do you want to save the global glossary and command changes*. It says nothing about style changes.

Use Format Styles Define.

❶ Select Format Styles(Alt-T Y).

❷ Select Define (Alt-D).

❸ Select Add to Template (Alt-E).

❹ Modify your styles, as you desire.

❺ If you are using NORMAL.DOT, when you close *WinWord* (or if you select File SaveAll), you will be prompted *Do you want to save the global glossary and command changes*. If you are using a different template, *WinWord* will ask whether or not you want to save changes to it. Ordinarily, the *Save Changes* prompt does not, by default, include changes to styles in the underlying template. However, since you explicitly turned that option on in the Add to Template checkbox, *WinWord* will save style changes to the template.

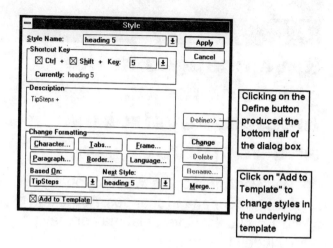

Clicking on the Define button produced the bottom half of the dialog box

Click on "Add to Template" to change styles in the underlying template

Save changes in the glossary, menu, macros, keystrokes, and ToolBar.

■ *WinWord* often offers to save global glossary and command changes. As indicated in Tip #90, however, that may or may not include style changes.

Use File Save All to save global changes.

When *WinWord* offers to *Save global glossary and command changes*, that includes all user customization to the keyboard, menus, ToolBar, macros, and commands. Similarly, any time *WinWord* offers to save a specific template, LETTER.DOT, or REPORT.DOT, for example, it will save template-specific changes in the glossary, keyboard, menus, ToolBar, macros, and commands. Moreover, if styles were modified as described in Tip #90, changes in styles are changed, also.

❶ To save all changes to templates without closing *WinWord*, select File SaveAll (Alt-F E).

❷ Select Yes to any *Save global* and *Save changes to template* questions.

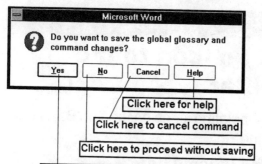

Microsoft Word

Do you want to save the global glossary and command changes?

[Yes] [No] [Cancel] [Help]

Click here for help

Click here to cancel command

Click here to proceed without saving

Click here to save changes in toolbar, menus, macros, glossary, keyboard, and any style changes made with the Add to Template option checked.

Add an icon to the ToolBar

■ Manipulating icons on the ToolBar is confusing.

Use the [space] item.

The ToolBar does not have Add and Delete commands. Instead, the ToolBar works on a *change* principle. To add, you change a [space] or an existing tool to a new one. To delete, you change an existing tool into a [space]. You cannot remove [spaces]. In standard VGA display (640×480), you can display at most 26 icons at any given time (by placing all of the [space]s at the right end of the ToolBar). If you leave fewer than four [space]s, the right-most icons will be pushed off the screen to the right.

❶ To add an icon to the ToolBar, select Tools Options ToolBar (Alt-O O T or Double-Click in any space on the ToolBar). Note that the Change button is grayed-out so it cannot be pressed.

❷ Select the [space] or tool where you want to add an icon. Press Alt-T to select **Tool to Change**, then use the Up and Down keys to highlight either a [space] (to add an icon) or an existing icon (to replace it). Don't press Enter at this time, and don't click the mouse on Close.

❸ Select Command (Alt-O) or Macro (Alt-M), depending on what you want to assign to the tool. If appropriate, select the context as well (Global or Template). Use the Up and Down keys to highlight the name of the command or macro you want to be associated with the tool.

❹ Select Button (Alt-B), and use the Up and Down keys to display the icon you want to use.

❺ Note that the Change button is no longer grayed-out. Select the Change button either by clicking it with the mouse or by pressing Alt-A.

❻ If you want to make more assignments, repeat steps 2 through 5 for each change you want to make. Click the Close button with the mouse when you're finished.

At this time, you can use only the built-in icon buttons displayed in the menu. These include 68 icon-faces, ten numerals, 26 letters, and one blank button.

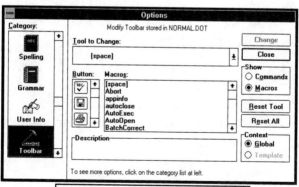

The Tool Bar has eight [space] slots on it. To add tools, you must replace the [spaces]s or existing tools.

Delete an icon from the ToolBar

- There is no delete command on the Tools Options ToolBar menu.

Tools cannot be deleted—they can be changed into other tools or changed into a [space].

You can effectively delete a tool by changing it to a [space], but that leaves a gap. There is no easy solution to remove the gap—you have to reassign every tool until the space works its way to the far right end.

➊ To remove an icon, select Tools Options ToolBar.

➋ Select Tool to Change (Alt-T).

➌ Highlight the tool you want to delete.

➍ Select Command (Alt-C).

➎ Select the [space] command (which really is no command at all).

➏ Select Change (Alt-A).

➐ Repeat steps 2 through 6 for each icon you want to zap. When you're finished, click on the Close button with the mouse (or tab to it and press Enter when it's selected).

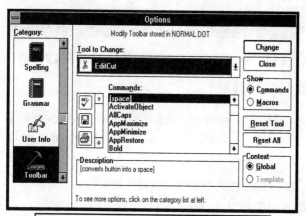

Select the tool you want to delete (EditCut shown here).
Select [space] as the command.
Click on Change.

Make macros run more quickly

■ Macros sometimes run slowly, especially when significant document scrolling is required.

Cut the macro's work by maximizing the screen

❶ Maximize the *WinWord* window and the document window by clicking on the application and document **maximize** buttons.

❷ Select View and establish the following settings:

Draft—On

Ruler—Off

ToolBar—Off

Ribbon—Off

❸ Select Tools Options View and uncheck each of the individual options; set the style area width to 0, also.

❹ Select View Zoom Page Width.

Turning off editing and navigation aids—scroll bars, ToolBar, Ruler—maximizes the screen area, reducing the frequency with which *WinWord* must redraw the screen. Invoking draft view and removing special markers and symbols reduces the complexity of each screen redraw.

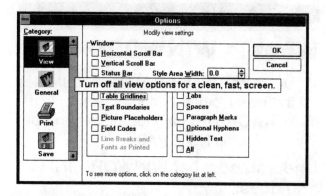

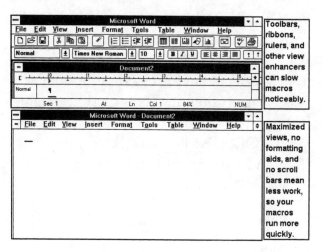

Toolbars, ribbons, rulers, and other view enhancers can slow macros noticeably.

Maximized views, no formatting aids, and no scroll bars mean less work, so your macros run more quickly.

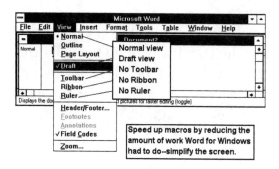

Speed up macros by reducing the amount of work Word for Windows had to do--simplify the screen.

What is WINWORD.INI?

■ Unlike WIN.INI, SYSTEM.INI, and .INI files for many other Windows applications, WINWORD.INI can't be edited and perused using NOTEPAD.

Understand what WINWORD.INI is and does.

WINWORD.INI is a structured binary file containing preferences and settings. WINWORD.INI is saved each time you Exit from *WinWord*, and is based on options you select while using the Tools Options menus. From the Tools Options menu, WINWORD.INI keeps track of your selections and settings in the following:

> View
> General
> Print
> Save
> Spelling
> User Info

Additionally, WINWORD.INI keeps track of the file cache (the list of up to four files that you see at the bottom of the File menu), as well as the last View settings (the View menu, as opposed to Tools Options View).

Force *WinWord* to offer alternative spelling suggestions

■ When *WinWord* finds a misspelled word, you may have to press Alt-S to force it to offer suggestions.

Turn on the Always Suggest option.

❶ Select Tools Options Spelling.

❷ Press Alt-S to check the Always Suggest checkbox.

❸ Press Enter.

There also are options to tell *WinWord* to ignore spelling irregularities in words in all uppercase and words containing numbers. Selecting these options speeds up the speller. Selecting Always Suggest slows down the speller. Take stock of the tradeoffs, and decide accordingly.

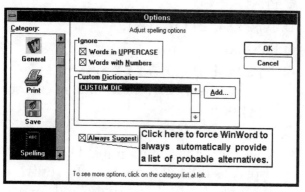

Make date fields display as "January 1, 1993" instead of "1-1-93"

■ When you select Insert Field and select Date, you include a format switch to force the date to display in full form. But, the default format is numeric. Most offices prefer the full form as the default.

Change the DATEFORMAT setting in WIN.INI.

❶ Select Tools Options WIN.INI.

❷ Press Alt-A (Applications).

❸ If the Application is not shown as Microsoft Word 2, then use the cursor Up and Down arrows to highlight Microsoft Word 2 (or whichever version of *WinWord* you're using).

❹ Press Alt-O (Option).

❺ Type **DATEFORMAT**.

❻ Press Alt-E (Setting).

❼ Type **MMMM D, YYYY** exactly. Ms must be upper case; the D and Ys can be upper or lower.

❽ Press Enter, twice.

❾ Now, fields that contain just Date will display as the full form date. To verify this, press Ctrl-F9, type **date**, and then press F9.

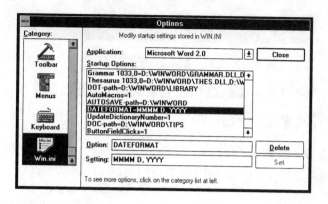

Make the Insert key do what it did in MS Word for DOS

■ In Word for DOS, the Insert key was used to insert text from the scrap. *WinWord*, however, subscribes to the Clipboard paradigm, in which you use Shift-Insert. Insert itself toggles between Insert and Overstrike mode. Users accustomed to using Insert in Microsoft Word for DOS should not be forced to form new habits in a word processor as smart as *WinWord*.

Set the Insert=Paste option.

❶ Select Tools Options General.

❷ Press Alt-U to check the Use INS key for Paste option.

In *WinWord*, the Clipboard is conceptually equivalent to DOS Word's Scrap. The step shown above only makes the Insert key mimic DOS Word's behavior—it doesn't change the behavior of the Delete key.

You would be well-advised **not** to try to get *WinWord* to emulate Word for DOS. The CUA (common user access) keystrokes are common across all Windows and OS/2 applications. Once learned, they are intuitive and useful. But, if you really want *WinWord* to thoroughly emulate Word for DOS's Scrap, you'll have to work at it. The Insert, Delete, and Shift-Delete keys can be reassigned using

Tools Options General (Insert) and Tools Options Keyboard. However, you cannot use either of these methods to assign Alt-F3 to EditCopy. Instead, you would have to write a macro.

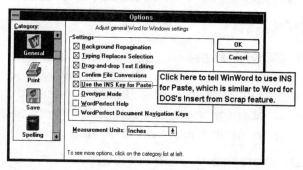

Default Assignments in WinWord and Word for DOS

Action	Command	WinWord Key	DOS Word Key
Copy to Clipboard	EditCopy	Ctrl-Insert	Alt-F3
Delete to Clipboard	EditCut	Shift-Delete	Delete
Insert from Clipboard	EditPaste	Shift-Insert	Insert
Delete without using Clipboard	EditClear	Delete	Shift-Delete

Tell *WinWord* to measure formatting in points

■ *WinWord* specifies some measurements in inches, and others in points. While you can specify the measurement units you want for any given setting, *WinWord* always seems to revert to inches.

Change the global default.

❶ Select Tools Options General.

❷ Press Alt-M (Measurement units).

❸ Using the Up and Down keys, highlight **points**, or whatever other units you prefer.

❹ Press Enter.

This action sets all horizontal units and some vertical. In Format Character and Format Paragraph, line spacing and character heights remain as LI and PT, respectively.

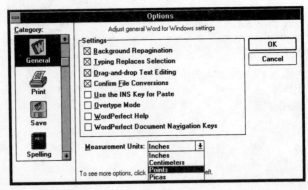

Don't try to reassign the cursor keys

■ Using Tools Options Keyboard to make assignments to the cursor pad keys doesn't seem to work. In fact, you can't even assign them using a macro.

Don't bother trying to reassign the following keys. *WinWord* won't let you.

Up
Down
Left
Right
Escape
Page Up
Page Down
Home
End

Print user-customized key assignments

■ When you make custom key assignments, it's easy to forget what you've done.

Print out your assignments.

❶ Make sure printer is turned on and is on-line.

❷ Select File Print (Alt-F P).

❸ Select Print (Alt-P).

❹ Highlight **Key Assignments** by pressing the Down key four times.

❺ Press Enter.

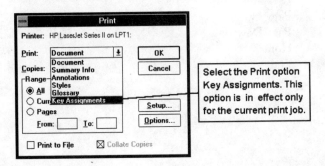

Select the Print option Key Assignments. This option is in effect only for the current print job.

Learn more about using *Word for Windows*

■ The User's Guide and Help system for *Word for Windows* 2 are much better than they were for earlier versions, but they don't answer every question.

Check out some of these sources.

When the User's Guide and online help system fall short, or when you crave a new perspective, turn to these sources for more information.

❶ *101 Essential Tips for Microsoft Windows*, by Clifton Karnes, 1992, Compute Books.

❷ *Word for Windows Revealed*, by Herbert L. Tyson, 1991, Windcrest/McGraw-Hill.

❸ *Word for Windows Companion*, Mark Crane, Microsoft Press.

❹ "The Working Word," "Lab Notes," *PC Magazine* (regular columns that frequently feature *Word for Windows*).

❺ MSWORD forum (GO MSWORD), CompuServe (call 1-800-848-8990 for information).

Index